Terence Fisher

MANCHESTER
UNIVERSITY PRESS

BRIAN MCFARLANE, NEIL SINYARD *series editors*

ALLEN EYLES, PHILIP FRENCH, SUE HARPER,
TIM PULLEINE, JEFFREY RICHARDS, TOM RYALL
series advisers

already published

Jack Clayton   NEIL SINYARD

Lance Comfort   BRIAN MCFARLANE

J. Lee Thompson   STEVE CHIBNALL

Terence Fisher

PETER HUTCHINGS

Manchester University Press

MANCHESTER AND NEW YORK

distributed exclusively in the USA by Palgrave

The right of Peter Hutchings to be identified as the author of this work has been asserted by him in accordance with the Copyright, Designs and Patents Act 1988.

Published by Manchester University Press
Oxford Road, Manchester M13 9NR, UK
and Room 400, 175 Fifth Avenue, New York, NY 10010, USA
www.manchesteruniversitypress.co.uk

Distributed exclusively in the USA by
Palgrave, 175 Fifth Avenue, New York,
NY 10010, USA

Distributed exclusively in Canada by
UBC Press, University of British Columbia, 2029 West Mall,
Vancouver, BC, Canada V6T 1Z2

British Library Cataloguing-in-Publication Data
A catalogue record for this book is available from the British Library

Library of Congress Cataloging-in-Publication Data applied for

ISBN 0 7190 5636 5 *hardback*
   0 7190 5637 3 *paperback*

First published 2001

10 09 08 07 06 05 04 03 02 01   10 9 8 7 6 5 4 3 2 1

Typeset in Scala with Meta display
by Koinonia, Manchester
Printed in Great Britain
by Bookcraft (Bath) Ltd, Midsomer Norton

Contents

List of plates

Series editors' foreword

The aim of this series is to present in lively, authoritative volumes a guide to those film-makers who have made British cinema a rewarding but still under-researched branch of world cinema. The intention is to provide books which are up-to-date in terms of information and critical approach, but not bound to any one theoretical methodology. Though all books in the series will have certain elements in common – comprehensive filmographies, annotated bibliographies, appropriate illustration – the actual critical tools employed will be the responsibility of the individual authors.

Nevertheless, an important recurring element will be a concern for how the oeuvre of each film-maker does or does not fit certain critical and industrial contexts, as well as for the wider social contexts, which helped to shape not just that particular film-maker but the course of British cinema at large.

Although the series is director-orientated, the editors believe that a variety of stances and contexts referred to is more likely to reconceptualise and reappraise the phenomenon of British cinema as a complex, shifting field of production. All the texts in the series will engage in detailed discussion of major works of the film-makers involved, but they all consider as well the importance of other key collaborators, of studio organisation, of audience reception, of recurring themes and structures: all those other aspects which go towards the construction of a national cinema.

The series will explore and chart a field which is more than ripe for serious excavation. The acknowledged leaders of the field will be reappraised; just as important, though, will be the bringing to light of those who have not so far received any serious attention. They are all part of the very rich texture of British cinema, and it will be the work of this series to give them all their due.

Acknowledgements

Over the lengthy gestation of this book, a number of colleagues and friends have made my life a lot easier by helping to track down rare Fisher films, reading through sections of the manuscript, digging up film stills, etc. So thanks go to Elayne Chaplin, James Chapman, Steve Chibnall, Sheldon Hall, Mark Jancovich, Eugene Karnstein (don't ask) and George Larke. Thanks too to my two editors Brian McFarlane and Neil Sinyard, and to Matthew Frost at Manchester University Press for his almost limitless patience.

Stills from Hammer Films are reproduced by kind permission of Terry Ilott at Hammer Film Productions Ltd. Thanks also to Ron Halpern and John Herron at Studio Canal *Plus*. Other stills are courtesy of the British Cinema and Television Research Archive. Stills from *The Curse of Frankenstein*, *Dracula* and *The Mummy* had unfortunately to be retracted as the book went to press, due to prohibitive permission costs. Every effort has been made to trace the copyright owners of illustrations; any person claiming copyright should contact the publisher.

Introduction

This is a book about the British film director Terence Fisher. A prolific film-maker with fifty titles to his credit, Fisher's last film – *Frankenstein and the Monster from Hell* – was released in 1974, when I was twelve. I was not old enough to see any of the horror films upon which Fisher's reputation rests when they were first released; for a number of them, I was not even born. I have been fortunate to see most of them in the cinema since, thanks largely to the National Film Theatre and the now sadly defunct Paris, Coventry, a cinema which in the early 1980s regularly showed Hammer horror double-bills on Sunday afternoons (along with other off-the-wall oddities such as a double-bill of *The Way We Were* and *Force Ten from Navarone*). However, my first encounter with the work of Terence Fisher was not in the cinema at all but on television. During the 1970s, BBC TV took to showing double-bills of horror films on Saturday nights through the autumn. The first half of the double-bill was usually a Universal horror film from the 1930s or 1940s, the second half a Hammer horror, directed more often than not by Terence Fisher. I remember being more interested in the Hammers than the Universals, mainly, I think, because the Hammers were in colour and, despite their period settings, seemed altogether more modern. I'm sure that I was aware of the seismic changes occurring elsewhere in the horror genre in this period. The release of *The Exorcist* in 1973 and *The Texas Chainsaw Massacre* in 1974 (incidentally, the same year that saw the release of *Frankenstein and the Monster from Hell*) finally confirmed what had gradually been becoming apparent throughout the 1960s – namely that American horror had gone contemporary and become very disturbing. But as I was not old enough to see any of these American horrors on their first release, my awareness of them at the time was necessarily rather distant.[1] (I would not become a fully paid-up member of the cinema-going horror audience until the slasher boom of the late 1970s.) Any history of horror which concerns itself only with 'cutting edge' developments in the genre misses out on this fact, that horror films persist in our culture long after their production, via TV, repertory schedules and, more recently, video and DVD, and that at any one time there are different entrance points into the genre. I know from my own experience that my encounter with those BBC horror double-bills is one shared by many of my age and nationality. For me, as for so many others, the 1970s belonged to Hammer horror more than it ever did to the likes of *The Exorcist* and *The Texas Chainsaw Massacre*.

Because of my interest in Hammer horror, Terence Fisher was one of the first film directors whose work I actively sought out. I knew very little about him other than that he made gothic horrors, but I liked what I saw. The films were not frightening but they were thrilling, suspenseful and endlessly fascinating. Given that from the early 1970s onwards – precisely when I was first seeing these films – Fisher was being identified by various critics as someone whose work exemplified peculiarly British traditions in British cinema and British culture generally, it is interesting that, so far as I can recall, my own relation to these films did not function at all in terms of their nationality. I didn't like them because they were British, I liked them because they were horror films.

My developing interest in Terence Fisher's films in the years since first seeing the likes of *The Curse of Frankenstein* and *Dracula* has been intertwined with and dependent on the way that British film history has developed over the past two decades. Thanks to the large number of books and articles about British cinema that are now available, I am much more aware of the industrial and social circumstances in which Fisher directed his horror films; I have also become familiar with the range of films – more than half of his total output – that Fisher made before he became associated with horror. In a sense, what has happened is that for me Fisher has been transformed from a horror director into a British director who in the second part of his career specialised in horror.

To a very large extent – and perhaps unsurprisingly for a book in a series entitled 'British Film Makers' – this is the perspective on Fisher adopted by what follows. I seek to offer a picture of the whole career rather than just a section of it. At the same time, however, I am not prepared to abandon entirely my earlier perception of Fisher as the horror-master. The kind of hesitation I am experiencing – between thinking about Fisher in the context of a specifically British culture and thinking about him as a figure whose work is not necessarily defined by or contained within national borders – is arguably apparent in certain features of Fisher's career itself. On one level, he is clearly a quintessentially British film-maker. Virtually all his films were made for British companies by predominantly British casts and crews, and usually in British studios. But a closer inspection makes the attribution of 'Britishness' seem less straightforward.

For example, Hammer, Fisher's base for much of his career, is now usually thought of in vaguely patriotic terms as a great British film company, but an awareness of the way in which it actually operated in the 1950s and 1960s quickly renders problematic any view of it as a purely and uncomplicatedly British enterprise. Like many 'independent' film companies, Hammer was in fact heavily dependent on American finance and was consequently always attentive to the needs of an American market. Both before and during its turn to horror production, Hammer had put a great deal of effort into forging a business relationship with the American film industry. The first tangible outcome of this had been a 1951 deal with American producer Robert Lippert; this had resulted in a procession of ageing and/or fading American stars featuring in the support features Hammer was producing at the time. (Incidentally, the first product of the Lippert deal was *The Last Page*, Terence Fisher's debut film for Hammer.) Later, the initial impetus for making a Frankenstein film came not from Britain but from America. American producer Milton Subotsky took his idea for a new up-to-date Frankenstein to Eliot Hyman at the New York-based Associated Artists Pictures who then presented the idea to Hammer in England. After producing a screenplay that was quickly rejected by Hammer, Subotsky took no further part in the production (although a few years later he settled in England and helped to establish Amicus Films, Britain's number two horror company in the 1960s and early 1970s). The resulting production of *The Curse of Frankenstein* was part-financed by Associated Artists Pictures and distributed by the American major Warner Brothers. Following *Curse*'s success, Hammer then quickly signed deals with both Universal and Columbia, thereby confirming its status as one of the first British companies to embrace the American film industry rather than viewing it as a threat. It seems from this that, in economic terms at least, Fisher's films were not as wholly British as they might at first have appeared.

Another way of establishing Fisher's work (and particularly the horror films) as significantly British is through locating it in relation to an indigenous gothic tradition. Novels as diverse as Mary Shelley's *Frankenstein*, Robert Louis Stevenson's *The Strange Case of Dr Jekyll and Mr Hyde* and Bram Stoker's *Dracula* stand as the best-known testaments to an apparently innate British propensity for macabre fictions. Such an approach has proved compelling and productive (although David Pirie, its main exponent, errs in referring to an English gothic tradition when so many of the major gothic writers are either Irish – Stoker, Charles Maturin, J. Sheridan LeFanu – or Scottish – Stevenson, James Hogg),[2] and it is certainly true that many of Fisher's films from the 1957–1962 years – notably *The Curse of Frankenstein*, *Dracula*, *The Hound of the Baskervilles* and *The Two Faces of Dr Jekyll* – stemmed originally from 'classic' British novels. Yet the degree of faithfulness to the original exhibited by these films turns out to be extremely limited, and it can in fact be argued that it makes more sense to see them instead as further variations on the influential American adaptations of these tales that appeared in the 1930s and 1940s (and which themselves were often more reliant on earlier stage adaptations than they were on the original literary texts). If the other early

Hammer horrors are then taken into account, the picture becomes yet more complicated. *The Mummy* is a weird pot-pourri of elements from previous Universal-produced *Mummy* films, *The Curse of the Werewolf* comes from a novel written by an American, and *The Phantom of the Opera* derives from a French novel (and also owes more than a passing debt to the two previous American-produced versions of the tale).

Hammer – and Fisher's horror work for the company – emerges from this as a patchwork or impure enterprise, a Frankenstein-like composite of British, European and American parts. To a certain extent, this reflects the nature of horror film production generally which since the 1930s has always had an international dimension. For example, while most horror production in the 1930s was based in Hollywood, the films made there often drew upon non-American sources (notably *Dracula* and *Frankenstein*) and also showcased the work of non-American film-makers such as, to give but two examples, the British director James Whale and the German cinematographer and director Karl Freund. (Perhaps the best-known example of this is *The Bride of Frankenstein*, the classic 1935 Universal production in which most of the cast and key members of the crew were British.) Later, during the 1950s, when horror production itself became more international with activity in Britain, Italy and Spain (and with Hammer the market leader in this process), there was still a constant movement of films, personnel and ideas between nations.

Of course, this does not mean that the question of national identity is unimportant, but it does need to be recognised that 'Britishness' is not some stable essence waiting to be discovered in its various manifestations by perceptive critics. Instead it exists as a set of ideas and discourses that circulate within a number of different contexts and which are subject to contestation and endless renegotiation. A revealing exchange of views about 'Britishness' – and one especially pertinent to an understanding of Fisher's work – occurred during the pre-production of *The Curse of Frankenstein*, Fisher's first horror film. Eliot Hyman, one of the film's American backers, wrote to James Carreras, the head of Hammer, about his concern that the film might prove too British for the American market. He acknowledged that the cast would be entirely British but commented that 'there are British casts and British casts ... although the people themselves may be British, just how British are they by way of an accent'. Carreras's reply was to the point: 'Reference cast, rest assured that the British cast will be absolutely first class and will have no trace whatsoever of British accent.'[3] There is an element of absurdity to this exchange, with a wily Carreras fobbing off a worried American financier with a reassuring but ultimately meaningless statement. At the same time, it is interesting how fluid and context-specific the notion of Britishness is in this exchange. (One also presumes that 'Britishness' here in fact means 'Englishness'.) At what point, in what way and for whom does a British cast become 'too British'? The urgency of Hyman's question has nothing really to do with national difference in the abstract but rather involves perceptions of national difference as they might impact upon the marketability of films in America. Ironically, and despite Hyman's concern, this Britishness arguably helped to differentiate Fisher's films, and the Hammer horror product in general, from its generic competitors (to the extent that some Italian film-makers adopted British-sounding pseudonyms to make their period horror films appear more like Hammer films).

Yet this is only one sense of Britishness, namely Britishness as it exists in the market for horror. As we have seen, the relation of Fisher's horror films to other contexts of Britishness – the British film industry, the British gothic tradition – is potentially quite complicated. Simply to reduce these films to being a singular expression of some quintessential feature of British national identity ignores the ways in which important aspects of their production and distribution cut across national borders (and, as we will see, this applies to much of Fisher's non-horror work as well). Nevertheless, the idea of Fisher's films speaking with a British accent is an appealing one. They might not be 'purely' British (whatever that might mean) but they are influenced, moulded and inflected by various notions of Britishness. One can choose to ignore this – as I ignored it on first viewing the horror films – but I believe, and I hope this book will demonstrate, that an appreciation of Fisher's films is aided by thinking about them in terms of that British accent. Ultimately, perhaps, this provides the best way of trying to understand what it is about Fisher's films that makes them so distinctive, and it takes us closer to explaining why some of these films have captured the imagination of so many for so long.

Notes

1 For the benefit of readers unfamiliar with the British film classification system, throughout the 1960s and 1970s most horror films were given an X certificate (since renamed an 18 certificate) which meant that no children were permitted entry.

2 See David Pirie, *A Heritage of Horror: The English Gothic Cinema 1946–1972* (London, Gordon Fraser), 1973.

3 Quoted in *The House that Hammer Built*, 1 (1997), p. 52.

1

Fisher in context

Career overview

So far as his career in cinema was concerned, Terence Fisher was always something of a latecomer. He did not enter the film industry until he was twenty-nine years old, he did not become a film director until he was forty-three, and he did not direct his first horror film (the type of film upon which his reputation was built) until he was fifty-two. To a certain extent, he was also a latecomer in terms of critical recognition; the first major study of his films – David Pirie's *A Heritage of Horror* – was published in 1973, a year after Fisher, who was then sixty-nine, directed his final film. Despite this 'tardiness', however, and as if to make up for lost time, Fisher was an extremely prolific film-maker who between 1947 and 1973 was responsible (usually as sole credited director, on a few occasions as co-director) for fifty films, an eclectic mix of melodramas, comedies, thrillers, science fiction and horror.

There was nothing about Fisher's early life that suggested a film-maker's vocation. He was born in London on 23 February 1904. Educated in Horsham, Sussex, he left school at sixteen to join the Merchant Navy. There he remained for the next five years. On leaving the Merchant Navy, and apparently for want of anything else to do, he went into the retail trade. In 1933 he was employed as a film clapper-boy at Lime Grove Studios in Shepherd's Bush, a ridiculously junior post for someone of his age (as Fisher himself often acknowledged in interviews.) Fisher spent the next three years as a clapper-boy, third assistant director and assistant editor, working at both the Shepherd's Bush studio (which was owned by the Gaumont-British company) and the Islington Studio (the home of the Gainsborough company which at that time was itself owned by Gaumont-British). In 1936 Fisher became an editor with the film *Tudor Rose*; he went on to edit a wide range of films – from comedy vehicles for Jack Hulbert and Will Hay to *The Wicked Lady* (1945), one of the more controversial Gainsborough melodramas – for a number of different studios and companies – the aforementioned Gainsborough, Warner Brothers (at their British Teddington studio) and Columbia-British. His last credit as editor was in 1947 with *The Master of Bankdam*.

The same year also saw the release of Fisher's directorial debut, the supernatural comedy *Colonel Bogey*. This 51-minute film was made at Highbury Studio, which at that time was run by the Rank Organisation and used as a showcase for new untested talent both before and behind the camera. Fisher remained at Highbury for two more films, one of which – *To the Public Danger* (1948) – was to become one of the better-known of his pre-horror films. He then graduated to full-length features back at Gainsborough which by this stage had also come under the control of Rank. Between 1948 and 1950 Fisher completed the post-war melodrama *Portrait from Life* (1948), the portmanteau drama *Marry Me!* (1949), the Noel Coward vehicle *The Astonished Heart* (1949) and the costume drama *So Long at the Fair* (1950) – the last two co-directed with Antony Darnborough.

Gainsborough ceased operation in the early 1950s and Fisher – whose work up until this point had not achieved much success, commercial or critical – found himself cast out into the low-budget sector of the film industry which throughout the 1950s and early 1960s was mainly concerned with the production – perhaps churning out might be a more appropriate term – of short genre films designed to support a main feature. Between 1951 and 1957 Fisher directed nineteen such films, the majority of these crime thrillers with a couple of science fiction films (*Four Sided Triangle, Spaceways*) and one rural comedy (*Children Galore*) thrown in for good measure. As had been the case with his previous work at Highbury and Gainsborough, Fisher's films from this period received virtually no critical attention at the time of their release, and Fisher himself remained an anonymous figure not readily distinguishable from other low-budget specialists such as Francis Searle and Charles Saunders. However, there was something about Fisher's career in what might be termed his 'wilderness years' that, while of no apparent importance at the time, would in retrospect become significant. Of the nineteen low-budget films directed by Fisher up until 1957, eleven were for a small, up-and-coming independent production company called Hammer.

Hammer's horror production represents one of the most striking developments in post-war British cinema. From 1957 onwards, a series of colour period horrors emerged from Hammer's Bray Studios which managed to upset (and occasionally delight) critics and, in the main, achieved huge box-office success. Many of these were directed by Fisher – including virtually all of the important earlier films such as *The Curse of Frankenstein* (1957), *Dracula* (1958), *The Revenge of Frankenstein* (1958), *The Mummy* (1959) and *The Hound of the Baskervilles* (1959). For a while, up until the box-office flop of *The Phantom of the Opera* in 1962, he was Hammer's main director. After that time he worked for the company less often, although returning occasionally to direct some of Hammer's more distinguished later films – notably *Frankenstein Created Woman* (1967), *The Devil Rides Out* (1968) and *Frankenstein Must be Destroyed* (1969).

The importance of Hammer horror to Fisher's career is indisputable. Of the twenty-three films he directed from (and including) *The Curse of Frankenstein* onwards, eighteen were made for Hammer, and sixteen of these were colour period horrors. (Another, the black and white *The Stranglers of Bombay*, is to all intents and purposes a horror film; the eighteenth film was a Robin Hood story, *Sword of Sherwood Forest*.) Fisher's importance to Hammer is equally indisputable; he was one of the key contributors in the initial formation of the type of horror upon which Hammer's subsequent success was built.

Apart from his films for Hammer, Fisher's later work included three science fiction invasion films – *The Earth Dies Screaming* (1964), *Island of Terror* (1966) and *The Night of the Big Heat* (1967)

– a German-produced Sherlock Holmes project, *Sherlock Holmes and the Deadly Necklace* (1962), and the horror-comedy *The Horror of it All* (1964). From the late 1960s onwards, his career was hampered by ill-health and other misfortunes; bizarrely, he was knocked down by cars on two separate, unrelated occasions, first in 1968 and then in 1969, breaking the same leg each time. Fisher directed his last film – Hammer's *Frankenstein and the Monster from Hell* – in 1972. By this stage the sort of gothic horror with which he had become firmly associated was out of fashion. The fact that *Frankenstein and the Monster from Hell* had problems securing a British distributor and was not released until 1974 speaks volumes in this respect. New forms of cinematic and literary horror were emerging in this period; the more explicit representation of violence and sexuality, along with a general suspicion of social authority, apparent in American films such as *The Exorcist* (1973), *It's Alive* (1974) and *The Hills Have Eyes* (1977) seemed far better suited to the cynical and somewhat paranoid mood of 1970s audiences than did the more ordered and by this stage rather cosy world-view offered by Hammer. Hammer itself would only release two more horror films after *Frankenstein and the Monster from Hell* – the Hong Kong-produced *The Legend of the Seven Golden Vampires* (1974) and *To the Devil ... A Daughter* (1976), both of them obvious, and ultimately unsuccessful, attempts to 'update' the Hammer format in the light of new trends at the box-office.[1]

Fisher himself played no part in this late, rather desperate activity. Given the miserable and depressed state of the British film industry throughout much of the 1970s, nor were there any opportunities for a film-maker of his type to work elsewhere. Accordingly, Fisher spent his latter years quietly in Twickenham, London, where he died on 18 June 1980.

Bugging it about a bit

I'm only a working director. (Terence Fisher)[2]

It would be hard to imagine a film director more modest and self-effacing than Terence Fisher. In his infrequent interviews, he always seemed to prefer discussing matters of technique and the everyday, mundane business of getting films made rather than making any grandiose statements about his films' content or about any ideas he might have wanted to express. When he was confronted with readings of his work which did seek to identify him as a film-maker with a distinctive authorial vision, Fisher's response is quite revealing. He is obviously flattered but at the same time somewhat uneasy: 'a director shouldn't speak for his films, they should speak for themselves. It is no good going into a long spiel of intellectual bullshit about why you do things or why you don't – the only thing that can speak is what you've actually directed, and all you've directed is a visual interpretation of the written word and perhaps bugged it about a bit – given it a few more guts in one direction or few less in another.'[3] Film direction here becomes 'bugging it about a bit', where 'it', presumably, is the script. Fisher was always insistent that the script, the written word, came before all else in film-making: 'For God's sake, the script is your Bible! It's the guts that you start with. All a director is, please, is an interpreter of the written word, or translator of the written word, into a visual form. Consequently, if the written word is no bloody good, no director in the world is going to be able to put it into a visual form which is going to be done ably.'[4]

This hardly seems the voice of a great film artist, someone described by David Pirie as one of the few British film directors whose films 'embody a recognizable and coherent Weltan-schauung'.[5] It is worth mentioning here that one of the initial impulses behind the study of directors as authors as it was developed in France in the 1950s was the perceived need to raise the status of the director above that of the screenwriter. As the individual who was most obviously in control of a film's visuals, the director came to embody in much authorship writing from the 1950s onwards that which was 'cinematic' as opposed to that which was 'literary'.[6] In assigning primacy to the script, and apparently subordinating his own directorial input to it, Fisher seems to be resisting or even refusing the designation of author or 'auteur' which Pirie, and a number of other British critics, have sought to bestow upon him. Worse still, Fisher's remarks appear to lend credence to the oft-expressed idea that British cinema is in some way more 'literary' than it is 'cinematic'.

Of course, not all critics and film historians believed that Fisher should be seen as a distinctive authorial presence in British cinema. For almost his entire film-making career, Fisher received virtually no critical attention at all (aside from some auteurist work done in France); Pirie's book did not appear until 1973, only a year before Fisher's final film *Frankenstein and the Monster from Hell* was released. Even the critical furore that greeted the first appearance of Hammer horror in the late 1950s tended to focus more on the studio than on the films' director. In addition, those critics who have spent time on Fisher are by no means united in praise. For David Thomson, Fisher and other Hammer film-makers seem 'like decent men who tended the garden on weekends'. On Fisher's work in particular, he writes 'the invention in the films seems fitful, desperate, and cynically detached from the genre'.[7] For Duncan Petrie, 'Fisher's view of the world is trite and reactionary, his style turgid and stagey',[8] while for Robin Wood 'Fisher is certainly consistent – the consistency being mainly a matter of unremitting crudeness of sensibility. The most striking thing about the world he creates is its moral squalor. His characters have no aliveness, no complexity. His conception of evil is scarcely more interesting, or more adult, than his conception of good: all is ugliness.'[9] To put it mildly, there is some dispute as to Terence Fisher's status as a film director. Is he an author with a distinctive and meaningful style and set of themes, or is he a hack (with Fisher himself apparently more comfortable with the latter designation)? Is he a moralist, as Pirie would have us believe, or an exploiter of 'moral squalor'? There does not appear to be any obvious middle ground here, no shared space within which one might negotiate a consensual position.

This is all quite striking given that Fisher's reputation, such as it is, rests almost entirely on his involvement in what in its time was one of the more vulgar, controversial and shocking developments in British cinema – the Hammer horror film. Critically shunned at the time of their initial release, Hammer horror films have been re-evaluated in recent years and now tend to be seen as belonging to a vibrant tradition of fantasy in British cinema, a tradition which also includes, amongst other things, the films of Tod Slaughter, Gainsborough melodramas, the films of Powell and Pressburger, and the *Carry On* series. It has often been argued that British cinema's 'fantasy wing' functions as a challenge to and disruption of the critically privileged realist tendency in British film. Fisher himself emerges from this as someone whose work is potentially a transgressive expression of that which is inexpressible elsewhere in British cinema.

There are some issues here which merit further discussion. For one thing, what is the precise significance of realism and fantasy in British film, and how can these concepts aid an under-standing of Fisher's work? One might also ask at this point how valid it is to think of Terence Fisher as an author-director – as we have already seen, Fisher probably has as many detractors as he has critical champions. There is a broader question here, how-ever. Given that film-making is a collaborative and industrial enterprise, how appropriate is it to bestow authorial significance on any individual, be it director, producer or screenwriter? Answering this will necessarily involve thinking about the role of the director in the British film industry. What we need to do here is explain some of the professional and industrial contexts in which Fisher operated and see how these relate both to the films he made and the way in which these films have been judged and valued.

Realism, fantasy, genre

It has long been a commonplace of British film criticism that British cinema has distinct traditions of realism and fantasy, and that it is the realist tradition which up until recently has received all the critical plaudits and dominated discussions about what it is that makes British cinema worthwhile. By way of a contrast, the fantasy tradition, while often popular with audiences, has in general been critically repudiated or ignored. In its cruder renditions, this way of seeing can transform British film history into a kind of relay race – with the realist team featuring John Grierson and his 1930s documentarists, the World War Two feature film-makers who were influenced by documentary, the British New Wave/ Kitchen Sink directors, Ken Loach, etc; and on the fantasy team Gainsborough melodrama, Powell and Pressburger, *Carry On* films and, not least, Hammer horror. Historical development becomes here little more than passing the baton from one set of films and film-makers to another. Much more productive has been the idea that realism and fantasy (or non-realism or anti-realism) are concepts that permeate and have an organising force within British cinema and British film culture while not necessarily dividing up British films into two rigidly demarcated camps.

There are still problems with the realism/fantasy dichotomy, however. For one thing, there is the question of nomenclature. If a film is not realist, is it non-realist, anti-realist or fantasy? Sometimes these terms are used as if they are more or less interchangeable, but each does carry its own distinct meaning. 'Non-realist' simply means different from realist, while 'anti-realist' implies an assault of some kind on the precepts of realism. Fantasy can be a vaguer term; it can refer to escapist or exotic entertainments, but in literary theory it has acquired a distinctive 'anti-realist' tenor. As Rosemary Jackson states: 'The fantastic traces the unsaid and the unseen of culture: that which has been silenced, made invisible, covered over and made "absent" ... literary fantasy is a telling index of the limits of that order. Its introduction of the "unreal" is set against the category of the "real" – a category which the fantastic interrogates by its difference.'[10] To a certain extent, it is this sense of fantasy that informs 'The Lost Continent', Julian Petley's influential account of British cinema's non- or anti-realist tradition. Petley argues that fantasy films 'form an other, repressed side of British cinema, a dark, disdained thread weaving the length and breadth of that cinema, crossing authorial and generic boundaries, sometimes almost entirely invisible, sometimes erupting explosively, always received critically with fear and disapproval'.[11] Petley invests this fantasy tradition with a libidinal energy that disrupts the polite, restrained decorum of realism with scenes of vulgar, sexualised excess. Such an approach tends to view British cinema as possessing a kind of psychical economy; in a Freudian sense, its dreams/nightmares (i.e. its horror films) and its jokes (i.e. its *Carry On* films and other vulgar comedies) provide access to its unconscious, revealing that which is repressed and/or inexpressible elsewhere. As one of Britain's main horror directors, Terence Fisher thereby becomes one of the gatekeepers of the cinematic unconscious, and his films themselves acquire a certain transgressive force.

This is a very dramatic way of conceptualising British cinema. Ultimately, perhaps, it is too dramatic; the horror-like scenario it conjures up of fantastic monsters lurking in the darkness, liable at any moment to crash through fragile doors and windows and assault the timid realists within, presupposes a too violent opposition between realism and fantasy. In a different context, Alan Lovell has criticised what he sees as a tendency in some British film criticism to pose restraint and excess as opposing forces. Lovell has written of his own disappointment on seeing some Gainsborough melodramas. A preparatory reading of plot summaries had suggested 'extravagant plotting and characterisation', but, according to Lovell, in the films themselves these elements 'were downplayed and made safe by the writing, camerawork, acting and direction'.[12] Lovell asks why it is that melodrama – or the horror films or comedies also in the fantasy tradition – should necessarily be free of the restraint and reticence apparent elsewhere in British cinema (and which has been seen by other critics as a defining feature of British film). He goes on to suggest that it might be more interesting to consider the ways in which realist restraint and fantastic excess interact with each other within particular films. Unfortunately, the only examples he cites are strong auteurist projects – namely David Lean's *Brief Encounter* (1945) and Michael Powell and Emeric Pressburger's *The Small Back Room* (1949) – and one does not really get any sense of how this approach might be applied systematically to British cinema as a whole.[13] Similarly, Robert Murphy's claim that the 'ethos of realism which was to be so important to the British New Wave is unexpectedly evident at Hammer'[14] is intriguing but arguably poses more questions than it answers. What exactly is the relation between realist and non-realist elements within Hammer horror (and the British New Wave, for that matter)?

As is probably clear by now, the terms 'realist' and 'anti-realist/ fantastic' have acquired a certain mobility in British film criticism. Not only have they designated trends within British cinema but they have also been used to describe tensions and interactions within specific British films. Matters are rendered yet more complicated when one realises that cinema itself as an institution can be seen as having, on a very fundamental level, a fantastic and a realist character; fantastic because cinema is a medium founded on illusion, on still, two-dimensional images being projected in such a way that an illusion of movement and depth is created; realistic because of cinema's reliance on the photographic reproduction of reality and on its eliciting an audience's assent (albeit a limited assent) to the 'reality' of what is being shown. As Andrew Higson has pointed out

> Clearly, different films, and particularly different genres of film mark themselves as *more* realistic, or *more* 'fantastic' (this is particularly evident in British film culture), but it needs to be recognised that such marking is always in relation to a particular understanding of cinema, a particular critical discourse, a particular sense of realism. All dominant cinema, all 'classic realist texts' work as fantasy for the spectator, but at the same time they make greater or lesser claims on our rapture and credibility, continually playing on this thrilling tension between believing that the diegetic world is real, and recognising that it is fantasy, between seeing the fiction as present and recognising it as absent.[15]

The mechanism outlined by Higson involves an audience knowing that what they are seeing is an illusion while at the same time believing in the 'realness' of the fiction, with this applying equally to films in the 'realist' and the 'fantasy' tradition.

One then needs to consider what the relationship might be between this very broad understanding of the function of fantasy and realism within cinema and the more localised and specific deployments of realism and fantasy within particular films or groups of films. Is there a relationship at all? If not, then perhaps we should not be using the same terms for very different things. If there is, some sense is required of what it is that might mediate between the realist and fantastic qualities of cinema as an institution and, say, Hammer horror or Gainsborough melodrama or the British New Wave.

It is in this context that a notion of genre can be very helpful. Particular genres can be seen as organising both an audience's belief (and disbelief) and interactions between realism and fantasy within films. A key concept here is neither realism nor fantasy but rather verisimilitude. In an important article dealing with genre theory, Steve Neale has defined verisimilitude as referring to 'various systems of plausibility, motivation, justification, and belief ... It entails notions of propriety, of what is appropriate and therefore probable (or probable and therefore appropriate)'.[16] Neale points out that what is appropriate and probable in one genre might not be so in another. So, one would expect song and dance numbers in a musical but not in a horror film. Similarly, one would anticipate certain types of violence in horror or war films which would be out of place in a comedy (although, as ever in discussion of generic types, one can always think of exceptions to 'the rule'). Using concepts developed by Todorov, Neale also distinguishes between various generic regimes of verisimilitude and a cultural/social verisimilitude; the latter is a discourse (or discourses) designating what we, 'the public', believe to be true. Obviously, there can be significant disparities between specific generic verisimilitudes and a cultural verisimilitude – for example, audiences are willing to accept people bursting into song, with full orchestral accompaniment, in musicals and supernatural phenomena in horror films even though they would not generally expect to encounter or even countenance the existence of such events in 'real life'.

As Neale indicates, those genres which deviate less from a cultural verisimilitude tend to have a realist quality. However, all genres elicit a particular sort of belief that what is happening in the genre is in some way 'real'. In horror, for example, one often finds characters who function as disbelievers and who in a sense are the voices of cultural verisimilitude. In the case of Fisher's work, one thinks of *Dracula*, in which Arthur Holmwood (Michael

Gough) does not believe in vampires, and *The Mummy*, in which Joseph Whemple (Raymond Huntley) does not believe in the existence of an ambulatory Mummy. As the films proceed, these disbelievers are made to believe, to accept a generic verisimilitude over a cultural one (in Whemple's case, with fatal consequences). Arguably, the anticipated triumph of the generic verisimilitude contributes to the genre's pleasurability. Belief and disbelief become part of the drama, with each genre managing this relationship in its own way.

When seen from this perspective, the issue of whether a genre can be seen as 'transgressive' – as Fisher's horror work has sometimes been seen as transgressive – requires some reconsideration. Transgression itself has become a somewhat overworked concept in film criticism, and one which has often lent itself to a facile equation of formal or thematic transgressiveness with a broader ideological transgressiveness. It needs to be recognised that what might be transgressive so far as a cultural verisimilitude is concerned could be, and usually is, an uncontentious and normative feature of a generic verisimilitude. It can also be said that genres develop historically via a constant series of small transgressions of their own norms as each genre film works to distinguish itself in limited ways from other films in the same genre. As far as Hammer horror was concerned, for example, probably its major generic transgression had little to do with its controversial representation of sexuality or violence but was simply the fact that it was in colour while the majority of earlier horrors had been in black and white.[17] Similarly, while, as noted by Robert Murphy, Hammer might have been 'realist' in relation to some of the more expressive 1930s horror films produced at Universal Studios, it was also relatively stylised in comparison with the American teen-horror films which started appearing at the same time as Hammer. These American horrors – which included *I Was a Teenage Werewolf* (1957), *I Was a Teenage Frankenstein* (1957) and *How to Make a Monster* (1958) – had contemporary settings (as opposed to Hammer's period settings) and were filmed in a 'flat' visual style. They were also in black and white when black and white signified a certain sort of realism.[18]

So where does this leave realism and fantasy? Clearly such terms lend themselves to a variety of uses, with these uses not necessarily forming a cohesive unity. At the same time, and especially as far as British film is concerned, 'realism' and 'fantasy' are indispensable, not least because of the important roles they have played in critical debates about British cinema. What would be helpful here – and for an understanding of Fisher's films it is probably essential – is a greater awareness of context when deploying such terms. When we discuss the 'realism' or 'fantasy' elements discernible in Fisher's films (and it's worth noting here that Fisher also worked in more 'realist' genres – notably the crime thriller), we need to specify clearly in relation to which structures or sets of beliefs – generic or cultural – these terms are operating. Furthermore, we should assess any claim for Fisher's 'transgressiveness' in the context of the particular generic histories to which his films belong rather than simply judging Fisher against some more abstract model of social or cultural propriety.

Directors and authors

As indicated above, there is some division between critics as to whether Fisher should be seen as a film artist or author whose work expresses a personal vision. Much of the negative criticism of this idea of Fisher as auteur clearly derives from critics thinking that he is simply not a good enough film-maker in comparison with other more 'legitimate' auteurs, e.g. Alfred Hitchcock, Orson Welles. There is something lacking in Fisher's work, it seems; lacking in the view of the world presented and/or in the use of filmic technique. Another criticism that might be levelled at Fisher's auteur status is more general, however, and involves taking issue with the very idea of the 'auteur-director' as an index of value in the study of film. How useful is it to see films in terms of a director's authorship?

'Auteurism' emerged as an important concept in film criticism in France during the 1950s. It was associated most of all with the journal *Cahiers du Cinema* and a group of young critics who would later themselves become film directors of some significance – namely, François Truffaut, Jean-Luc Godard, Claude Chabrol, Eric Rohmer and Jacques Rivette. *La politique des auteurs*, the approach favoured by *Cahiers* in the 1950s, involved identifying, and indeed praising to the heavens, film-makers who had managed to produce a body of work which in some way or other was an expression of the artist's distinctive view of the world. The most contentious aspect of this approach was *Cahiers'* insistence that the auteur was always the director, not the screenwriter who had previously laid strong claim to being a film's author. The reasoning behind this privileging of the director was that as the person most responsible for a film's visuals or mise-en-scene, the director was more in touch with what was 'cinematic' as opposed to what was 'literary'. *Cahiers* also made an important distinction between the auteur and the metteur-en-scene – the auteur, as we have seen, was the artist-director whose personality manifested itself in his work; the metteur-en-scene, by way of a contrast, was the sort of director who serviced the script without imposing his own artistic imprint upon it. (Interestingly, some of the comments from Fisher quoted above about his approach to his work sound more like those of a metteur-en-scene than those of an auteur.)

Auteurism's history within film criticism has proved to be a chequered one. Given that this history has been covered in detail elsewhere, I don't intend to go through it again here.[19] Suffice it to say that for all auteurism's initial contentiousness, looking at cinema in terms of directors has now become commonplace in film criticism. Newspaper and television film reviews routinely assign significance to whoever has directed a particular film; and a glance at the film section of any bookshop quickly reveals that director studies are an important feature of published writings on the cinema. At the same time, within the more confined world of academic film studies, 'auteurism' is generally perceived as a rather old-fashioned way of thinking about film, one long since superseded by more relevant and exciting approaches.

One of the main criticisms of an exclusive focus on the director as source of cinematic meaning and value is that it precludes a proper consideration of the creative input into cinema of other professions, e.g. scriptwriters, cinematographers, production designers, editors, etc. Film-making is a collaborative process, after all, and surely critical accounts of cinema should take account of this fact. In the case of Terence Fisher in particular, the horror films he directed for Hammer between the late 1950s and the mid-1960s (less so his later Hammer work) are characterised by a remarkable consistency in terms of the creative personnel participating in their production; producers Michael Carreras and Anthony Hinds, writers Jimmy Sangster and John Elder (the latter a pseudonym for Anthony Hinds), cinematographer Jack Asher, editor James Needs, production designer Bernard Robinson, composer James Bernard, as well as, of course, actors such as Peter Cushing and Christopher Lee are, in various combinations, involved in virtually all of Hammer's horrors up until the mid-1960s. How reasonable is it then to maintain that the distinctive character of Fisher's Hammer horror films is mainly to do with him rather than deriving from a collaboration between the various members of the 'Hammer team'? Put like this, it is clearly not reasonable at all, and it is precisely for this reason that some film historians prefer to think about companies and studios as entities which themselves, in a sense, 'create' the movies that emerge from them. As Pam Cook puts it, 'studio histories can provide a useful antidote to accounts of cinema history that confer agency and power on charismatic individuals or groups. They remind us that film-making is a collaborative process subject to cultural and economic forces. They encourage us to view style as the end result of a series of negotiations between managerial, creative and technical personnel, rather than the realization of a single personal vision.'[20] Here notions of personal authorship are seen as mystificatory, obscuring the economic realities of film production.

One of the principal benefits of auteurism in its initial 1950s manifestation was its 'discovery' of artistic value in Hollywood cinema, a cinema which up until that time had not generally been thought of in such terms. However, the way in which auteurists did this – by finding auteur-directors working within Hollywood – has since been criticised for its reliance on some very traditional aesthetic values and methods, and especially its promotion of the idea of the uniquely talented, visionary artist. It has been argued that this emphasis has hindered a consideration of how cinema might be different from older, more established cultural forms. 'This implicit acceptance of the dominance of the traditional arts was strengthened by the use of the auteur theory which used the common critical tool of traditional artistic criticism (the author expressing the personal vision).'[21] One might say here that while taking Fisher seriously as an auteur-director might well bring more clearly into view British horror, a cycle of films that has been critically despised and/or ignored through much of its history, it also separates Fisher out from the cycle through stressing how exceptional he is. Horror is thereby rendered interesting only because Fisher is working within it; it is of little interest in itself.

A neglect of the collaborative contexts within which film production takes place, and a reliance on what might be termed 'elitist' concepts of artistic value: both these factors seem seriously to undermine the credibility of looking at film in terms of directors. As if this were not damning enough, there are also some more localised problems involved in thinking about Fisher in particular as an auteur (apart, that is, from the aforementioned question of whether he is good enough). Most notably, the stress laid in much auteurist criticism on the necessary cohesiveness of an auteur's body of work, on the way in which an auteur's films can be linked together thematically and stylistically, does not sit easily with the overall shape of Fisher's career in British cinema. Claims for Fisher as a distinctive film-maker relate almost entirely to his work in the horror genre from 1957 onwards, and yet these films comprise less than half of his directorial output. What is one to do with the mix of thrillers, comedies and melodramas that make up Fisher's non-horror work? One possibility, the logical auteurist one, is to link them with the better-known horror films and argue that they are all equally expressive of an authorial vision. Another possibility is to ignore these non-horrors; as most of them precede Fisher's horror films, one might argue that they represent journeyman work done prior to Fisher's finding his authorial 'voice' in the horror genre. From an auteurist perspective, this is a much riskier prospect for it threatens to undermine any sense of coherence in a film-making career. If Fisher is not an auteur all the time, then perhaps he is not an auteur at all.

As it turns out, most previous accounts of Fisher as a film-maker of note have tended to steer a course between these two possibilities, finding intimations of horror in his early films without feeling the need to consider systematically the non-horror work as a whole.[22] So films that have a generic affinity with Hammer horror (e.g. the science fiction films *Four Sided Triangle* and *Spaceways*) or anticipate it thematically (e.g. the costume melodrama *So Long at the Fair*, even Fisher's editorship of the Gainsborough melodrama *The Wicked Lady*) are invoked, while the low-budget thrillers that constitute the bulk of the early part of Fisher's directorial career are rarely mentioned.

Given that this is a book dealing with Terence Fisher, it should be obvious that I want to treat Fisher as a film-maker who in various ways is distinctive and noteworthy, and that this will inevitably involve some sense of there being qualities apparent in a range of Fisher's films that can ultimately be assigned to his creative agency. At the same time, some of the more traditional 'auteurist' approaches to directors do not necessarily provide the best way of addressing and evaluating Fisher's career. The auteur/metteur-en-scene dichotomy, with every director having to be one or the other, is particularly unhelpful. It can spur critics into producing absurdly inflated readings of films in order to avoid casting their chosen director into the ignominy of metteur-en-scenedom. Conversely, in the case of established, canonical auteurs, it can also induce a certain critical complacency, with every detail of every auteur film automatically seen as resonating with authorial significance.

As noted above, one possible solution to the apparently intractable set of problems posed by 'auteurism' is to abandon it altogether and move on to other approaches. However, while the business of film-making is undoubtedly collaborative, one needs to note that it is also highly organised and hierarchical. Some professions have significantly more input than others, and throughout much of the history of cinema the director has been an especially privileged figure in this respect.[23] It follows that to avoid the question of the director's role and contribution leads inevitably to a neglect of an important factor in the production process. Of course, this is not the same as saying that directors are creative agents or artists, but it does address the industrial contexts within which questions of creativity can more profitably be considered.

A key assumption underpinning auteurist writing is that all directors – be they auteurs or metteurs-en-scene – are more or less the same in terms of the industrial function they perform. In fact, it is this very consistency in 'job description' that permits a comparison between and ranking of particular directors. For example, one can reasonably compare directors Alfred Hitchcock and Michael Curtiz and on the basis of this comparison claim that Hitchcock's films are more 'personalised' than those of Curtiz. Comparing Hitchcock with a screenwriter or a cinematographer is more problematic because the people involved are doing different jobs. However, the industry itself has not always been so obliging in providing consistent job descriptions for the directors working within it.

To give a specific example of this from British cinema, one can compare Terence Fisher with David Lean. Lean had one of the most prestigious and glittering careers of any post-war British film director (although, perhaps because of the international nature of his later films, he has been a somewhat marginal figure in recent debates about the nature and value of British cinema). There are actually a few parallels between Fisher and Lean: both debuted as directors in the 1940s, both had previously been editors, and both worked with Noel Coward early in their directorial careers – Lean with *In Which We Serve* (1942) – which was co-directed by Coward as well as written by him – and the Coward-written *This Happy Breed* (1944), *Blithe Spirit* (1945) and, most famously, *Brief Encounter* (1945); Fisher with *The Astonished Heart* (1949), which was written by and starred Coward and was co-directed by Antony Darnborough. Yet Fisher and Lean's positions within the British film industry were strikingly different. In the 1940s Fisher worked first at Highbury and then at Gainsborough; both of these (like much of British cinema at this time) were owned by the Rank Organisation. Gainsborough in particular can be seen as a producer-centred organisation where the director was given less leeway than was the case elsewhere in British cinema. (In fact, Fisher's entire career was spent working in set-ups which privileged the producer, not least at Hammer.) By contrast, Lean sought to acquire a position of control and power within the industry. In interviews Fisher described himself as a director for hire; one suspects that this was the last thing Lean wanted to be seen as. He, along with film-makers such as Frank Launder and Sidney Gilliat, Michael Powell, Emeric Pressburger and Ronald Neame, were involved in setting up Independent Producers at Rank in the early 1940s; this was an initiative that gave the film-makers concerned far more control over their projects than, say, the film-makers working at the Rank-owned Gainsborough.

It seems from this that the term 'film director' has to be stretched quite considerably to encompass both Fisher and Lean. While they might both carry the job description 'director', their respective positions within a hierarchical production process lead to their having different levels of involvement in and control over budgets, choice of projects, script development, casting, and access to technical resources in production and post-production. In a sense, they are doing different jobs. Arguably, this difference also has an impact on the way in which the films concerned are critically received. Lean's films were likely to be taken more seriously because Lean had claimed for himself the position of independent, free artist within the film industry; regardless of the qualities of individual films, they came from a sector of the industry that demanded a certain critical attention and respect. Fisher's films, by way of a contrast, carried no such aura of importance and, again regardless of their qualities, were less likely to be taken seriously. (Interestingly, more recent critical accounts of British cinema have tended to invert this. Almost as a matter of principle, that which is perceived as coming from the 'underside' of British film production is praised at the expense of an official British film culture seen as conservative and meretricious.)

I have deliberately avoided here the question of whether Lean is more or less talented than Fisher. Obviously, judgements about films and film-makers need to be made at some point; however, such judgements are more readily based on a knowledge of the circumstances in which said films were produced. A certain flexibility in evaluative criteria is required as one moves, say, from an expensive and prestigious period drama to a Hammer horror film, or from Lean's work to Fisher's. This does not mean that one type of film or film-maker is inherently superior to another and that one has to relax standards for the lesser; merely that they are different, and that a proper assessment of them needs to register and take account of that difference.

It follows that a discussion and evaluation of Fisher's films needs to be matched to precisely where he was in the industry when directing them. Such an approach certainly helps to explain some of the changes in direction in Fisher's oeuvre as he moves from one part of the industry to another, from one type of film-making to another. Within the traditional auteurist method, such changes constitute something of a problem inasmuch as they endanger any idea of perfect authorial coherence and consistency.[24] My feeling on this is that we should focus instead on the realities of the director's situation as he (or she) moves through the industry. In the case of Fisher, one can identify elements of continuity running through much (although by no means all) of his work. Even here, as an essential prerequisite to evaluating Fisher as a film-maker, one needs to gain a sense of how these elements are formed within and in relation to particular industrial and collaborative contexts. One also needs to consider those films which don't fit easily into what Fisher was doing elsewhere – an oddity like *Children Galore* (1954) for example – not in order to bring them via inventive readings into the Fisheresque authorial fold but instead to identify what sort of career it was that led Fisher into making these sorts of films. Admittedly, the critical approach this implies – one sensitive to direction as a profession rather than as an artistic vocation – is somewhat less dramatic than the auteurist model with its stress on the auteur heroically transcending the constraints imposed by a philistine film industry. This loss of drama is more than compensated for, I think, by a gain in detail and nuance. A case can certainly be made for Fisher as a film-maker who via the exercise of his professional skills within particular contexts helped to fashion films that in part (and, in some cases, in very large part) register his organisational presence within the production process. However, simply to abstract Fisher from the industry and place him in opposition to it is to do a disservice both to Fisher and to the industry that helped form him as a film director.

Having said all this, there are certain qualities of auteurism which perhaps merit further consideration and which militate against its outright rejection, with these stemming largely from its reliance on cinephilia. At the risk of oversimplification, cinephilia refers to a particularly intense way of seeing and experiencing film; the cinephile seeks out moments of epiphanic, quasi-mystical revelation within films, moments that uncover in some way or other the indefinable essence of cinema.[25] This revelatory relation-ship with cinema clearly underpins much auteurist writing in its concern to seek out and reveal the auteur's presence within particular films. On the basis of a cinephile experience of the cinema, auteurists have often fashioned what might be termed a phantasmic version of the auteur, with the relation of this to the real-life director involved not always straightforward. Some 'auteurs' – notably John Ford and Howard Hawks – always seemed uncom-fortable with auteurist readings of their work; others – most famously Hitchcock – were more interested and willing to engage with these readings in their subsequent professional activities.[26] In a late 1960s revision of auteurism, Peter Wollen argued that the critical uncovering of structures within films that might pertain to an authorial 'signature' should be bracketed off from the real-life intentions and activities of the auteur-director himself: 'Auteur analysis does not consist of re-tracing a film to its origins, to its creative source. It consists of tracing a structure (not a message) within the work, which can then *post factum* be assigned to an individual, the director, on empirical grounds. It is wrong, in the name of a denial of the traditional idea of creative subjectivity, to deny any status to individuals at all. But Fuller or Hawks or Hitch-cock, the directors, are quite separate from "Fuller" or "Hawks" or

"Hitchcock", the structures named after them, and should not be methodologically confused.'[27] Wollen was concerned to introduce an objective, even scientific, tenor into auteurism in order to counter what he saw as the impressionistic character of earlier auteurist writing. Yet Wollen's work, too, can be seen as betraying a distinctly cinephile attitude to its subject. The figure of the auteur, far from being a source of objective meaning, remains both a focus for and the phantasmic outcome of cinephile activity – it represents the end-product of many hours spent in the cinema, gazing raptly at the screen in search of that indefinable something.

Recent critical work on British cinema has had little time for this sort of cinephile activity. This is primarily because the main emphasis in this work has been a historical one. What one finds here is a wholly laudable and very productive concern with the histories of companies and studios, with the state's relation to the industry, with critical institutions and audiences' reception of films. Within such a context, cinephilia – which, if nothing else, is highly subjective and impressionistic – functions in a sense as the Other of history, as marking the point where historical method-ologies end and something else begins. Cinephilia speaks of a passion and a desire for film; cinema itself is figured as an experience that is both unique and mysterious. Film history by definition is concerned with contextualisation, with the placing of films within particular frameworks; for a cinephile there are no contexts, only the immediacy of cinema itself as a self-sufficient object. I raise this matter here for two reasons. First, and generally, an awareness of cinephilia can arguably clarify our sense of film as film, as a medium with properties peculiar to itself. Second, more particularly, because Terence Fisher is one of the few British film directors who seems to have acquired a cinephile following. This is most apparent in the French work on him but it also, I think, informs Pirie's *A Heritage of Horror*.[28] This book will focus on the historical Fisher, but at the same time it will retain an awareness of Fisher as the object of cinephile attention, mainly because, inevitably perhaps, its own analyses of Fisher's films are likely to be informed by a certain cinephilia. How does the cinephile's

Fisher, the phantasmic Fisher, relate to the director who for nearly thirty years worked quietly and modestly in the low-budget sector of the British film industry?

It seems to me that such an approach is essential to a comprehensive understanding of the sort of cinema represented by Fisher's work. The French film-maker and critic François Truffaut once famously (or irritatingly, depending on your perspective) stated that there was a certain incompatibility between the terms 'British' and 'cinema'.[29] British film critics have sometimes been overly concerned with what French critics think of British cinema; the British response to Truffaut, when not one of masochistic agreement, has been to assert the aesthetic richness, complexity and vitality of British film. Such a response arguably misses the point for Truffaut is speaking very much as a cinephile; and, for a cinephile, cinema is not valued because it is aesthetically interesting, it is valued because of the passion it invokes. Can one be passionate about Fisher's work (or British cinema in general)? This is not the sort of question that is usually posed within the paradigms and methods currently dominating the study of British film. At the same time it is surely an indispensable question as we set out to evaluate the films of Terence Fisher.

Notes

1 *The Satanic Rites of Dracula* (1973) – Hammer's final Dracula film – was produced after *Frankenstein and the Monster from Hell* but was released in Britain several months earlier.
2 Harry Ringel, 'Terence Fisher underlining', *Cinefantastique*, 4:3 (1975), p. 20.
3 John Brosnan, *The Horror People* (London, MacDonald & Janes), 1976, p. 112.
4 Ringel, 'Terence Fisher underlining', p. 20.
5 David Pirie, *A Heritage of Horror: The English Gothic Cinema 1946–1972* (London, Gordon Fraser), 1973, p. 51.
6 For a key example of such an approach, see François Truffaut, 'A certain tendency of the French cinema', *Cahiers du Cinema in English*, 1 (January 1966), pp. 30–40.
7 David Thomson, *A Biographical Dictionary of Cinema* (London, Andre Deutsch), 1994, p. 244.
8 Duncan Petrie, *Creativity and Constraint in the British Film Industry* (London, Macmillan), 1991, p. 15.

9 Quoted in S. S. Prawer, *Caligari's Children: The Film as Tale of Terror* (Oxford, Oxford University Press), 1980, p. 268.

10 Rosemary Jackson, *Fantasy: The Literature of Subversion* (London, Methuen), 1981, p. 4.

11 Julian Petley, 'The lost continent', in Charles Barr (ed.), *All Our Yesterdays: 90 Years of British Cinema* (London, BFI), 1986, p. 98.

12 Alan Lovell, 'The British cinema: the known cinema?', in Robert Murphy (ed.), *The British Cinema Book* (London, BFI), 1997, p. 239.

13 Charles Barr has suggested something similar to Lovell: 'Possibly the conventional binary opposition of realist and non-realist is a too rigid one.' He too refers to *Brief Encounter* – considered the epitome of realism when it first appeared – and the films of Powell and Pressburger – often viewed as leading anti-realists – as examples of an intermingling of realism and fantasy. Barr, 'Amnesia and schizophrenia', in Barr, *All Our Yesterdays*, pp. 15–16.

14 Robert Murphy, *Sixties British Cinema* (London, BFI), 1992, p. 164.

15 Andrew Higson, 'Critical theory and "British cinema"', *Screen*, 24:4–5 (July–October 1983), p. 91.

16 Steve Neale, 'Questions of genre', *Screen*, 31:1 (Spring 1990), p. 46.

17 Obviously, the introduction of colour would have had an impact on the ways that sexuality and violence were represented – but colour itself was the distinctive new feature.

18 As a gimmick, the conclusion of *How to Make a Monster* was filmed in colour. For a relevant and interesting discussion of the role of transgression within generic development, see Barbara Klinger, 'Cinema/ideology/criticism revisited: the progressive text', *Screen*, 25:1 (January–February 1984), pp. 30–44.

19 For a good account of authorship in film, see John Caughie (ed.), *Theories of Authorship* (London, Routledge/BFI), 1981.

20 Pam Cook, 'Introduction', in Cook (ed.), *Gainsborough Pictures* (London, Cassell), 1997, p. 11.

21 Alan Lovell, *Don Siegel: American Cinema* (London, BFI), 1975, p. 5.

22 Fisher biographer Wheeler Winston Dixon is an exception as he works through virtually all of Fisher's films, horror and non-horror. While admiring his diligence, I think that on occasions his attempts to connect these films leads to the neglect of other factors operative in their production. Wheeler Winston Dixon, *The Charm of Evil: The Life and Films of Terence Fisher* (Metuchen, NJ and London, Scarecrow Press), 1991.

23 Although this 'privilege' is not universally accepted and in fact has often been challenged, most notably by producers and screenwriters.

24 For more on this, see Peter Hutchings, 'Authorship and British cinema – the case of Roy Ward Baker', in Justine Ashby and Andrew Higson (ed.), *British Cinema – Past and Present* (London, Routledge), 2000, pp. 179–89.

25 For a discussion of cinephilia, see Paul Willemen, *Looks and Frictions: Essays in Cultural Studies and Film Theory* (Bloomington and Indianapolis, Indiana University Press), 1994, pp. 223–57.

26 See Robert E. Kapsis, *Hitchcock: The Making of a Reputation* (Chicago and

London, University of Chicago Press), 1992 for an interesting discussion of this.

27 Peter Wollen, *Signs and Meanings in the Cinema* 3rd edition (London, Secker & Warburg), 1972, p. 168.

28 For an example of French writing on Fisher (and one which contains bibliographical references to other French material on the director) see René Prédal, 'Anthologie du cinéma no. 109: Terence Fisher', *L'Avant Scene du Cinema*, 295/296 (1982), pp. 274–304.

29 François Truffaut, *Hitchcock* (London, Granada), 1978, p. 140.

2

Fisher before horror

A barred view

Fisher's horror work at Hammer from 1956 onwards finally bestowed upon his career a stability that up until then had generally been lacking. Before then – from *Colonel Bogey*, his 1947 directorial debut, through to his first horror film, *The Curse of Frankenstein* (produced in 1956, released in 1957) – Fisher had worked for a variety of different companies at different studios. A film-maker for hire, someone who had little or no choice regarding the projects upon which he worked; Fisher, in the 1947–1956 period at least, hardly seems a promising candidate for authorial status. For an auteurist of the old school, this, of course, would be grist to the mill; the auteur-critic, with his faith in the auteur's infallibility, seeks to demonstrate the ways in which the auteur has transcended the constraints imposed by the industry and produced works that stand as testaments to a particular personal vision. As argued in the previous chapter, such an approach generally obscures the material and industrial realities of film production. It is particularly inappropriate as an approach to Fisher in the 1947–1956 period; while there certainly are distinctive elements in Fisher's pre-1956 films, the body of work as a whole simply does not cohere together in a manner that lends itself to a traditional 'authorial' analysis. In other words, notable features that might reasonably be assigned to a recognisable directorial input relate to particular films and isolated moments within films rather than informing all or even most of the work for which Fisher was responsible in this period.

It could well be asked at this point – if this is the case, then why bother looking at these films at all in terms of their director? One answer is that there are individual films of merit here which are in part remarkable because of the way in which they are directed. Another is that Fisher's work in this period is significant inasmuch as it anticipates and helps to illuminate the later and more distinctive horror production at Hammer. This is certainly the case thematically – Fisher does seem drawn to those elements within particular films which will subsequently become key in Hammer horror – and industrially: Fisher's progress through various parts of the film industry and types of film-making can be seen to prepare him for the sort of film-making in which Hammer will specialise from the mid-1950s onwards. On these grounds alone, and so long as one does not make inflated auteurist claims for them, Fisher's early films merit consideration from the perspective of his contribution to them.

At the same time, it is useful to retain an awareness of how these films are different from the horror films to come, different both aesthetically and in terms of where they come from in the industry. This is partly because some of these films represent notable directorial achievements without necessarily anticipating horror. An overly teleological approach can obscure their significance and the way in which Fisher's career at this stage contains possibilities, not all of which are subsequently realised in the horror work. It is also because Fisher can be seen as a film-maker who constantly 'remakes' himself throughout his career, as he moves from editing to direction, from Gainsborough to low-budget independent production, from non-horror to horror, adjusting all the time to changes in the industry and his position within it. What this means is that, in a very fundamental way, his career lacks continuity, and any account of him as a film-maker needs to take this into account. It follows that, contrary to the dictates of a more traditional auteurist approach, those elements of continuity in Fisher's work in the 1947–1956 period (and there definitely are such elements) should be measured against and not prioritised over all the differences and discontinuities. The sort of approach this implies is best illustrated through a specific example, and the example I have chosen is *The Astonished Heart* (1949), Fisher's sixth film as director. Admittedly this is a rather perverse starting point: it is not a film for which any Fisher-auteurist has ever made any substantial claims and I myself am not inclined to value it very highly. The account of it offered here is intended instead to highlight both the benefits and some of the problems involved in thinking about Fisher's career generally in its pre-horror phase.

The Astonished Heart was a Gainsborough production. A rather gloomy melodrama, it deals with a psychiatrist (played by Noel Coward, who also wrote the screenplay) who has an affair with his wife's friend (the wife played by Celia Johnson, the friend by Margaret Leighton). Eventually the psychiatrist can no longer cope with the emotional and psychological turmoil caused by the affair, and he commits suicide by throwing himself off the roof of the block of flats where he and his wife live.

The Astonished Heart was not well received either critically or commercially on its initial release, and it has not fared well since: a recent account of British cinema simply described it as 'appalling'.[1] Such outright dismissal is unfair, I think. The film is certainly more interesting than this, with part of this interest (although by no means all) arguably relating to Fisher's input. One scene in particular is significant in this respect. It involves the moment when Chris (Noel Coward) kisses Leonora (Margaret Leighton) for the first time, with this taking place just inside the front door of Leonora's house. The camera looks down upon the lovers through the banisters of the first floor landing. This set-up puts the audience at a distance from the lovers and composition-ally puts the lovers themselves behind bars, trapped by the very desire which they think will free them. Exactly the same camera set-up is repeated twice later in the film; first, immediately after the affair has collapsed when a despairing, suicidal Chris is leaving Leonora's house for the last time; second, a few minutes later when we are shown the empty hallway, the door still left open after Chris's departure. On the soundtrack we hear a phone ringing as Chris's wife tries desperately and unsuccessfully to contact her husband. This repetition – and the association it sets up between the first kiss and the loss of self-control and ultimate self-destruction that it brings – expresses the fateful consequences of the psychiatrist's desire far more economically and effectively than does the film's somewhat verbose dialogue.

Anyone familiar with Fisher's later work, and especially the horror films, will recognise characteristic formal and thematic elements here. A frequent emphasis on static camera set-ups such as this, set-ups which are obviously designed with editing patterns in mind, arguably reflects Fisher's own background as an editor. In a similar way, the sequence in Fisher's 1968 film *The Devil Rides Out* in which the villain attempts to hypnotise someone deploys camera set-ups that are in themselves predominantly immobile but which are clearly meant to be edited together in a particular way in order to produce what in this case is a very effective dramatic tension.[2] Fisher has sometimes been accused of being an 'uncinematic' film-maker because he does not move the camera very much. It is worth pointing out that there are more ways of being cinematic than simply moving the camera, and in any event, as we will see, Fisher does move the camera rather more frequently than has sometimes been supposed.

In thematic terms, a sense of desire as a dangerously uncontrollable force can also be seen to inform Fisher's later films. In the horror work, the powerful and effective heroes tend to be celibate (notably Van Helsing in *Dracula* and Father Sandor in *Dracula – Prince of Darkness*) while those individuals who succumb to desire usually end badly (and in some cases become the villains of the films in which they appear). In the pre-horror work discussed in this chapter, one gains a sense that Fisher is more engaged in those scenarios which afford him the possibility of exploring or commenting upon the perils of desire. As Fisher was never a director who could pick or choose his projects, this goes some way to explaining the unevenness of the non-horror films. It might also help to explain the greater consistency of the horror films inasmuch as horror as a genre has always been drawn towards scenarios involving desire and sexuality.

Seen in this way, *The Astonished Heart* becomes one of those intimations of horror mentioned in the previous chapter, anticipating as it appears to do distinctive elements in Fisher's later, more accomplished work. However, even as I offer this as a reading of *The Astonished Heart*, I am aware of its selectiveness, of the way in which it suppresses or ignores other elements in the film. It is worth considering here whether the 'discovery' of Fisher in *The Astonished Heart* represents something significant or whether in fact it is just a case of a cinephile auteurist willing the chosen auteur into existence through overly inventive interpretations.

In his classic auteurist piece 'Notes on the auteur theory in 1962', the American critic Andrew Sarris, in a manner not entirely dissimilar to that adopted above for *The Astonished Heart*, describes how while watching *Every Night at Eight* (1935), an obscure Raoul Walsh film, he came across a scene – of the heroine watching the hero as he sleeps – which anticipated a similar scene in Walsh's later, better-known *High Sierra* (1941). Sarris writes 'If I had not been aware of Walsh in *Every Night at Eight*, the crucial link to *High Sierra* would have passed unnoticed. Such are the joys of the auteur theory.'[3] Sarris was quickly taken to task by fellow critic Pauline Kael for investing too much significance in what she inimitably refers to as 'a pathetic little link between two Raoul Walsh pictures', adding that Sarris 'never does explain whether the discovery makes him think the pictures are any better'.[4] The main target for Kael's invective is what she sees as the obscurantist and mystificatory elements apparent in auteurism; in other words, what she seems to be reacting against is cinephilia, its language and its emotion.

Bearing all this in mind, what exactly should the status be of a 'pathetic little link' between *The Astonished Heart* and Fisher's later films? An auteurist might well highlight particular, potentially authored elements within certain films and do so more effectively than other approaches. However, a considered judgement of the significance of such elements necessarily involves moving away from the cinephile's private realm and considering the specific production contexts within which the films in question were fashioned. *The Astonished Heart* is especially interesting in this respect inasmuch as it had one of the most troubled and complicated production histories of any of Fisher's films.

Originally *The Astonished Heart* was not to be directed by Fisher at all. Adapted from one of the ten single-act plays that in various combinations made up Noel Coward's *Tonight at 8.30* – another of the plays, *Still Life*, had formed the basis for *Brief Encounter* (1945), three more would be filmed for the portmanteau film *Meet Me Tonight* (1952) – it was due to star Michael Redgrave as the psychiatrist and to be directed by Anthony Asquith from a screenplay by Muriel Box.⁵ Asquith left the project before production began, the Box screenplay was replaced by Coward's own screenplay, and Fisher and Antony Darnborough became co-directors. Shooting began with Redgrave in the lead role but after two weeks, and apparently at the instigation of Coward himself, Redgrave was replaced by Coward. There is some disagreement as to why this happened: Coward's published diaries indicate that he simply thought Redgrave was not right in the role while Redgrave's autobiography suggests a certain amount of dithering on Coward's part as to whether he wanted to play the part himself – hence the delay in agreeing to do it.⁶

Peter Wollen has stated that those inputs in the film-making process that might potentially obscure a critical perception of authorial elements should be thought of as 'noise'.⁷ Seen in this way, *The Astonished Heart* is an especially noisy production, with Coward himself wielding considerable influence and Fisher not the sole director in any event. The latter presents a considerable obstacle for any auteurist reading of the film (although, given that film-making is collaborative, it really shouldn't). The strange thing about this is that the co-director in question, Antony Darnborough, spent most of his career in cinema as a producer (including the production of Fisher's earlier film *Portrait from Life*) and only notched up two directorial credits, both of them as co-director with Fisher, *The Astonished Heart* and *So Long at the Fair* (1950). It is not clear what exactly his role was as co-director of *The Astonished Heart* (for which he was also producer), but given his previous and subsequent film-making experience it seems reasonable to suppose that Fisher would have dealt with the more technical aspects of film direction – this, after all, was where his experience lay – while Darnborough dealt more with the actors. (Interestingly, Coward's own account of the production in his published diaries mentions Darnborough but not Fisher. Notes added by the diary editors mistakenly identify Sydney Box as the film's co-director. Given that one of these editors, Graham Payn, actually appeared in *The Astonished Heart* as the psychiatrist's assistant, this does not bode well for any substantial claims for Fisher's authorship.)[8] The repeated camera set-ups described above – where there is no dialogue and the camera is nowhere near the actors – can arguably be seen as 'technical' and therefore more likely to have been the result of Fisher's decisions than Darnborough's. The authorial possibilities apparent in those set-ups still stand, then, although they are now starting to look much more tentative. As is always the case when one engages with film-making as a collaborative enterprise, the imputation of authorship becomes both more complicated and delicate than it does in a more straightforward auteurist approach.

The input of Coward himself also merits some consideration, especially in the light of his previous involvement in *Brief Encounter*. It cannot be denied that in certain respects *The Astonished Heart* harks back to *Brief Encounter*; it comes from the same theatrical source, it features Celia Johnson and Joyce Carey, both of whom had appeared in the earlier film, and it tells a comparable story of thwarted love. In a provocative account of *Brief Encounter*, Andy Medhurst has argued that the film can in fact be seen as a tacit expression of gay desire represented via and rendered covert through an ostensibly heterosexual relationship, with this in turn relateable to Coward's own homosexuality. Such an interpretation flies in the face of more conventional and canonical readings of the film, and Medhurst himself worries about whether this reading has 'any substantive base in the text itself or is it only a collective fantasy, a shared "special thrill"?'[9] before concluding that there is a case to be made for Coward's gay authorship. Whether or not one accepts Medhurst's case for *Brief Encounter* (a film which has a substantial gay following), it does seem that in certain respects *The Astonished Heart* would make more sense as a narrative if the Margaret Leighton character were a man. As things stand, it is hard to comprehend what is so unnerving about the affair that the urbane and cosmopolitan psychiatrist feels compelled to kill himself. However, if we think of Leonora as Leonard, we can then factor in the public disgrace and the illegality of the affair. The idea of a desire that is scandalous, dangerous and destructive of one's peace of mind, that is in fact almost a disease or affliction, has a potentially gay dimension. Admittedly this relates to an idea of gayness that is both stereotypical and oppressive – it would be hard to see this film as progressive in this or any other respect – but it does throw an interesting new light on the psychiatrist's actions.

I would not want to push this reading too far, although I do think it successfully identifies tensions within the film that are not identifiable in any other way. The significant thing here is how distant such a reading seems from the sort of film-making associated with Terence Fisher. Horror as a genre has often been associated with non-conventional representations of gender and has attracted film-makers who are themselves gay and/or concerned to explore same-sex desire (in terms of British film directors, one thinks of James Whale and Clive Barker). In the face of this, Hammer horror, and Fisher's work in particular, emerges as overwhelmingly and resolutely heterosexual in its preoccupations and overall tone. For Fisher, desire – and this applies in the pre-horror work as well – is invariably heterosexual and, more often than not, male desire for the woman rather than vice versa. The composition in *The Astonished Heart* which puts a man kissing a woman behind bars can be seen as speaking in this respect of Fisher's investment in the narrative, in terms both of technique and of interpretation. Meanwhile the material which lends itself to a gay reading is communicated elsewhere, mainly in the dialogue written by Coward himself.

The Astonished Heart emerges from this as somewhat incoherent (reflecting perhaps its production history). Possible traces of Fisher's input are minimal, as one might expect from a project in which Noel Coward was so obviously the leading light. Thinking about the film in terms of Fisher can alert us to some of its dissonances and contradictions. More importantly for our purposes, looking at this film in this way can also benefit our sense of how Fisher develops as a director. I have already suggested on the basis of our knowledge of the film's production that Fisher might be seen as using the limited opportunities afforded him in *The Astonished Heart* to present a particular view of the drama: in his own words, he gives it some guts in a particular direction. To a certain extent, this can be seen as symptomatic of his directorial career throughout the 1947–1956 period as he intervenes sporadically and periodically into the projects that happen to come his way. The co-direction of *The Astonished Heart* introduces some uncertainty into the allocation of authorial responsibility – that barred composition might well have been Darnborough's or someone else's idea – but it is worth pointing out that such uncertainty is always present in film, regardless of what the directorial credit might read. At the risk of repetition, film-making is a collaborative enterprise and the assignation of responsibility for any element in it needs to be based on a sense of how the collaboration operates. It is too often assumed that an auteur-director has a totalising control over a film when this is not apparent in the film's actual production. For example, some accounts of Fisher's horror films have bestowed credit upon him for aspects of the films that demonstrably represent the input of the screenwriter, the production designer or the cinematographer.

So far as understanding the director's development is concerned, it is important to have some sense of how the director in question benefits from such collaborations, how he not only contributes to but also takes from the films with which he is associated. As for *The Astonished Heart*, discovering that the barred composition was in fact Darnborough's would be surprising given the known background to the film's production and Fisher's prior career. Even if it were the case, however, one might argue that Fisher had taken this view, and all that it represents, away with him and done interesting things with it in his later films. It is certainly the case that the barred view and an accompanying idea of desire as fearful and dangerous resonates throughout much of Fisher's most interesting work, including work done before *The Astonished Heart* (just as it is equally certain that it plays no significant part in Darnborough's subsequent work).

I earlier referred to Pauline Kael's disparagement of a moment of cinephile discovery. While sympathetic with her impatience at some of the language deployed by cinephile auteurists, I nonetheless think that such moments of discovery, of revelation if you will, can be useful. In particular they help us to identify organising elements within films, albeit elements which then, in various ways, need to be related back to how the films in question were actually made. This in turn can lead to a more measured assessment of Fisher's work before horror than that offered by a traditional auteurist approach concerned to protect the 'infallibility' of the auteur-director.

Fisher at Highbury and Gainsborough: 1947–1950

The years that Terence Fisher spent as a director at the Highbury Studio and at Gainsborough represented the last moment in his career when he would be employed by a large film company, namely the Rank Organisation which in the late 1940s owned both Highbury and Gainsborough. The seven films Fisher directed (or co-directed) there are remarkably, if not bewilderingly, divergent in terms of subject matter, generic identity, tone and level of accomplishment. There are certainly moments that are striking and noteworthy, and two remarkable films – *To The Public Danger* (1948) and *Portrait from Life* (1948) – but the overall impression one gains of Fisher in this period is of a film-maker who is technically proficient without being particularly distinctive, or at least not consistently distinctive.

As if to underline this, most of the films he directed at Highbury and Gainsborough were thoroughly conventional, both generic-ally and in broader aesthetic terms, and rarely went beyond the norms and types that characterise British cinema at this time. The two 'exceptional' films mentioned above – *To The Public Danger* and *Portrait from Life* – are interesting precisely because they are different; they stand apart from the conventional, especially so far as their respective subject matters are concerned. It is arguably this 'out-of-the-ordinary' quality that affords Fisher the opportunity, for two films at least, to become an out-of-the-ordinary director as, freed from the weight of convention and expectation, he seeks out the most appropriate cinematic means and devices for conveying these strange stories.

In large part the conventionality of Fisher's films in this period can be seen as a function of the industrial context within which he was working. This was particularly the case at Highbury, a very small studio in Islington, London, that before the war had been used mainly by independent producers but which had become part of the Rank Organisation after the war. In the late 1940s a series of short (45 to 60 minute) films were produced there, mainly to give untested personnel – especially the young actors who constituted what came to be known as 'the Charm School', Rank's training centre for new acting talent – experience of the film-making process. Budgets were low (£20,000 according to one source), schedules tight and technical resources were extremely limited.[10] Given these circumstances, it is not surprising that there is a certain conventionality in Fisher's films at the studio; there was simply not enough time, money and resources for them to be anything else.

Fisher's directorial debut *Colonel Bogey* (1947), for example, is a comic ghost story of a kind that British cinema regularly turned to in the 1930s and 1940s –with films such as *The Ghost Goes West* (1936), *Don't Take it to Heart* (1944), *Blithe Spirit* (1945) and *The Ghosts of Berkeley Square* (1947) as well as various comedies in which the ghosts turned out to be fakes, criminals or, if in wartime, Nazi spies, with the best-known examples of these being *The Ghost Train* (filmed in 1931 and 1941) and similarly themed Will Hay and Arthur Askey vehicles such as *Oh Mr Porter* (1937), *The Ghost of St Michael's* (1941) and *Back Room Boy* (1942).[11]

Fisher's take on this well-worn theme is set at the turn of the century and depicts a young couple attempting to rid themselves of the 'blimpish' ghost of Uncle James. There are some obvious gothic possibilities here – with the dead hand of the past weighing down upon the present – but as the film is a good-natured comedy, none of these are exploited. One might compare the film in this respect with 'The Haunted Mirror' episode of Ealing Studio's *Dead of Night* (1945) where another couple have their lives disrupted in a far more disturbing manner by a spectral force emanating from the past. Given his later association with horror, it is interesting that Fisher never worked in the more angst-ridden and psychologically aware tradition of the British ghost story, a tradition that finds its fullest expression in British film in *Dead of Night* and *The Innocents* (1961). Instead *Colonel Bogey* offers an amiable tall tale with its only surprise relating to its ending. In their final bid to get rid of Uncle James, the couple inform him that his old regiment is being deployed against the suffragette movement. An outraged James promptly sets off to haunt the regiment. This rare cinematic reference to female emancipation from this period can be seen as a late expression of a wartime egalitarianism. However, the film's ostensible support for the suffragette cause is qualified somewhat by its stereotypical representation of the suffragettes themselves.

By way of a contrast, *Song for Tomorrow* (1948), Fisher's third and final film at Highbury, does not even manage amiability. An unlikely romance involving a surgeon, a pilot, an opera singer and some amnesia, it sounds more interesting than it actually is (and it doesn't sound that interesting). A review of the time dismissed it as 'shoddy and insignificant'.[12] Probably its only point of interest is that Christopher Lee, Hammer's star-to-be and one of the Charm School's more unlikely graduates, makes a brief, negligible appearance.

Given the circumstances of its production, it is all the more remarkable that *To the Public Danger*, the film made by Fisher between *Colonel Bogey* and *Song for Tomorrow*, is as striking as it is. Of course, it shares many of the features of the other Highbury films – a short running length, a small cast, a minimal number of sets – but somehow these features here work to enhance the atmosphere of seediness and desperation that *To the Public Danger* seeks to convey. Described by one historian as 'an allegory about the longeurs of civilian life after six years of war',[13] its genesis, surprisingly, lies in a pre-war government road-safety campaign. As part of its support for this campaign, the BBC commissioned the writer Patrick Hamilton – famous for his stage plays *Rope* and *Gaslight* and the novel *Hangover Square* – to produce a radio play illustrating the dangers of drunk driving. Hamilton had good reason to respond with enthusiasm; in the early 1930s he himself had been knocked down by an allegedly drunk driver and left permanently disfigured as a result. The play *To the Public Danger* was broadcast in February 1939 and was a considerable success; Hamilton subsequently received appreciative letters of support as well as some hate mail (the latter presumably from outraged drunk drivers).[14]

To the Public Danger's narrative is simple enough. The slightly drunk Captain Cole (played in the film by Dermot Walsh) and his paralytically drunk friend Reggie (played rather improbably by Roy Plomley, creator and host of the BBC radio series *Desert Island Discs*) visit a roadside pub where they encounter a young couple, Fred and Nan (the latter played by Charm School graduate Susan Shaw). Nan is clearly attracted to Captain Cole who is a much more glamorous and exciting figure than the decent but dull Fred. Largely through Nan's efforts, she and Fred end up in Cole's car, being driven at speed by an increasingly drunk Cole. Inevitably, given the road-safety origins of the piece, the car hits what appears to be a cyclist. Fred wants to stop but the others talk him out of this. Later, spurred on by his sense of social responsibility and more tacitly by his jealousy over Cole's interest in Nan (and vice versa), Fred fights with Cole, gets away from him and the others and reports the accident to the police. The police quickly discover that Cole had in fact only hit someone's unoccupied bicycle. Meanwhile Cole, now erroneously convinced that the police are after him, drives even faster and more dangerously until the car crashes off the road and he, Nan and Reggie are killed.

With minimal resources, Fisher effectively conveys a sense of post-war ennui and aimlessness with violence lingering just beneath the surface. To a certain extent, the film might be seen as an example of film noir, especially in the way that it conjures up a world of anti-domestic impermanence, with most of the drama taking place in pubs and in speeding cars. At the same time, it is very British in its presentation of a society ridden with class division. Clearly part of Cole's 'glamour' for Nan resides in his middle-classness, and Cole's bullying of both Fred and the pub landlord derives from what he obviously sees as an innate class superiority. Fisher biographer Wheeler Winston Dixon is right, I think, to see Cole as an early version of the monstrous aristocrats who appear in Fisher's later Hammer films, notably Sir Hugo Baskerville in

The Hound of the Baskervilles (1959) and the Marques in *The Curse of the Werewolf* (1961).[15] However, Cole is an unusual figure within the context of 1940s British cinema; in his contemporaneity, his middle-classness and his unremitting self-destructiveness, he stands apart from the swaggering aristocratic bullies one finds in such 1940s Gainsborough melodramas as *The Man in Grey* (1943) and *Jassy* (1947). Fisher is aided immeasurably in this by Dermot Walsh's performance. Walsh had previously appeared as an amiable upper-class gent both in the costume melodrama *The Mark of Cain* (1947) and the aforementioned *Jassy*. By way of a contrast, here he manages to convey the sheer nastiness of Captain Cole in a wholly convincing and disturbing manner. Cole emerges as a comprehensively mean-spirited individual who has contempt not only for others but for himself as well. The moment where, just before the final crash, his near madness is accentuated by a low-angle close-up implies that his death is in fact a kind of suicide, one not motivated by any particular event in the film but nevertheless the logical endpoint for this type of character.

In the face of such intensity, the road-safety message – 'don't drink and drive' – becomes bathetic, and even the film's ostensible morality is unbalanced. Fred might well be the most socially responsible character but he is also the dullest. In addition, the film's attempts to make Nan culpable for some of the trouble – it is her desire for sensation that leads her to Cole, she is holding the wheel when they hit the cycle – do not convince. In part this is to do with the casting; one feels that Susan Shaw is just too nice to be like that. It is also because the focus of Fisher's attention is elsewhere, on the homme fatal Cole rather than the putative femme fatale Nan. To an extent, this sets a pattern for the later films where those female characters thought of as dangerous (the character played by Marie Devereux in *The Stranglers of Bombay*, Carla in *The Gorgon*, Christina in *Frankenstein Created Woman*, even the Diana Dors character in the earlier *The Last Page*) often turn out to be remarkably passive, their significance defined instead by the actions of men.

To the Public Danger is a considerable achievement but it is also something of a one-off, both for Fisher and for British cinema.

The boozy, despairing view of the world it offers is actually much more characteristic of Patrick Hamilton (who, aside from being the victim of a drunk driver, was himself an alcoholic of considerable magnitude) than it is of Fisher. What appears to have happened here is that for the first time in his career, Fisher was given a project that was in itself distinctive and interesting and which Fisher himself was able to present in a manner that both successfully conveyed and enhanced this distinctiveness.

Fisher's next professional engagement after working at Highbury represented a definite step-up in the industry so far as budgets, technical resources and running lengths were concerned. He moved to the Gainsborough company where he directed (or co-directed) four feature films. Given that Fisher had already worked at Gainsborough as an editor in the 1930s and 1940s, this was in fact a kind of return – especially so since *Portrait from Life*, the first Gainsborough film to be directed by Fisher, was made at Shepherd's Bush studio, the very studio where he had secured his first job in the film industry fifteen years previously. Having said this, Gainsborough in the late 1940s was quite different from Gainsborough as it had been when Fisher had worked there before. Throughout the war and in the immediate post-war period, Gainsborough had been very successful with a series of lurid costume melodramas (including *The Wicked Lady*, on which Fisher had been editor). By the time Fisher arrived to make *Portrait from Life*, the studio had taken a different direction under the control of Sydney Box. The rate of production had increased while budgets had generally decreased (with the exception of relatively expensive 'prestige' projects such as *The Bad Lord Byron* and *Christopher Columbus*); and the company was about to become involved in broader industrial difficulties that ultimately would see Gainsborough closed and Fisher himself with an apparently stalled career.

There are no signs of the trouble to come in *Portrait from Life* which is an extremely accomplished and interesting film. It deals with the attempts of various men to discover (or, in one case, conceal) the true identity of a young woman living in a displaced person's camp in Germany immediately after the war. The woman, first known as Hildegard but subsequently revealed to be Lydia, is played by Swedish actress Mai Zetterling who only a year before *Portrait from Life* had appeared in Ealing Studio's similarly themed *Frieda* (1947). In both, Zetterling plays a German who has to be rescued by an English male from the perils of Nazism, perils embodied in *Frieda* by Frieda's own fanatic brother and in *Portrait from Life* by Hendlmann (Herbert Lom), the Nazi officer who falsely claims to be Hildegard/Lydia's father as a way of concealing his own identity. In the case of *Frieda*, this takes on a symbolic resonance; saving Frieda is equated with rehabilitating Germany, redeeming it (or sections of it) from a Nazi past. At the same time the film also seeks to dissipate British post-war prejudices about Germans. *Portrait from Life* moves in quite a different direction; it turns out that Hildegard/Lydia is not German at all but an Austrian Jew, and the film itself displays little interest in how Germany should be perceived as a nation in the aftermath of war. Instead *Portrait from Life*'s convoluted narrative structure, while ostensibly centred upon the question of a woman's identity, is in fact much more about men and their problems. Like *To the Public Danger*, it has certain 'noirish' qualities, both visually and in terms of its depiction of a male neurosis which is never fully explained in the film but which seems to relate in some way to the experience of war. The drunken, despairing artist Duncan Reid in *Portrait from Life* features in this respect as a more humane but equally self-destructive version of the loathsome Captain Cole in *To the Public Danger*.

'None of this would ever have happened if Helen hadn't let me down.' These are the first words we hear in *Portrait from Life*. They are spoken by Major David Lawrence (Guy Rolfe), recently returned to Britain from the Army of Occupation in Germany. The Helen in question is the woman with whom he was planning to spend his leave only to find that she has just married. Clearly she is not the love of his life; he's not so much traumatised as mildly put out. He wanders through London for a while before ending up in an art gallery where, in an exhibition of work by war artists, he finds and is fascinated by Duncan Reid's portrait of Hildegard. 'I just couldn't take my eyes off her', his voice-over informs us, although the tone of this remark is uncertain. Lawrence's narration generally lacks the doomed, neurotic quality often associated with the male voice-overs found in some contemporaneous films noir. Instead it proceeds in a brisk, no-nonsense manner and the fact that Lawrence is speaking in the past tense implies that he has come through the events of the narrative relatively unscathed.

As Lawrence stares at the painting, an old man by the name of Professor Menzel appears by his side. The Professor claims that the painting is a portrait of his long-lost daughter Lydia whom he had to abandon while fleeing from the Nazis. Partly out of his own interest in the portrait and partly, one feels, for want of anything better to do, Lawrence agrees to help 'the old boy' (as he calls him) track down Duncan Reid, the artist responsible for the painting. Reid is quickly discovered in a drinking club. Unfortunately he is in the advanced stages of alcoholism and is dangerously ill. He dies before Lawrence and Menzel can learn more from him about the portrait. Lawrence subsequently returns to Germany where he sets out to find whether the woman in the portrait really is the Professor's daughter.

What follows sets up a kind of doubling relationship between Lawrence and Reid inasmuch as they both seek the truth about Lydia/Hildegard (with Reid's attempt conveyed in flashback form) and in doing this have to confront Lydia's false father, the villainous Hendlmann. In his classic account of the uncanny, Sigmund Freud has suggested that doubling offers a way of preserving the ego by splitting off undesirable elements and projecting them elsewhere, notably on to the double itself. At the same time, the existence of the double evokes paranoia as the boundary between self and Other is eroded. The double thus becomes an ambivalent figure, combining as it does both reassuring and threatening characteristics.[16] In the case of *Portrait from Life*, this doubling derives from a narrative structure in which the same story – the investigation of Lydia – is told twice but with different endings for each version, one tragic and the other happy. The parallels drawn by the film between Lawrence and Reid can be seen in this respect as part of the film's attempt to maintain a certain masculine stability and authority. However, even as *Portrait from Life* seeks to do this – by contrasting the strong man with the weak man – it is also haunted and to a certain extent structured by Reid's failure. Further anxieties accrue from the possibility that Lawrence is not quite the decisive figure he appears to be, that in certain respects he might not be that different from Reid.

By the time we get to the lengthy flashback dealing with Reid's efforts to save Lydia, we already know that he is dead; and certainly a sense of doom hangs over him in the flashback itself. 'I'm going to die,' he tells Lydia bluntly at one point, although why precisely he is dying is never made clear. Is this disease his alcoholism or some other fatal malady which has caused him to turn to drink? Elsewhere his drink problem is seen, albeit vaguely, as a depressive reaction to war that has not been dissipated by war's end. 'There is no war now', Lydia tells him. 'No, and there's no peace either for some of us', a self-pitying Reid replies. Clearly Reid does desire Lydia but it is a desire ridden with self-loathing and guilt. In particular, he feels guilty about the age difference between them. Not only is he thirty-one and she a mere eighteen but, as Reid informs her, because her memories of some of those years are missing, for him she is only thirteen or fourteen in terms of her experience of the world. Given all this, it is hardly surprising that Reid's final encounter with Hendlmann, when he threatens the German with a gun, ends with Reid's failure and his final decline into terminal alcoholism.

As we have already seen, Lawrence is apparently different, more confident, more in control of himself. His search for Lydia is, in part at least, motivated by a sexual curiosity; when someone enquires of the object of his search 'Supposing she was a hideous old hag with no teeth, would you still want to go?', Lawrence's slightly abashed reply is 'Well no'. However, his ultimate aim is to restore Lydia to her father, and he acts throughout as an agent for that father. This helps to explain the awkwardness of the film's conclusion. When Lydia, now rescued from Hendlmann, hints at the prospect of marriage to Lawrence, Lawrence's response is polite but less than enthusiastic. (Apparently this ending was tacked on in an attempt to make the film more up-beat. I have been unable to ascertain what the original ending was.) It seems that Lydia is not his but instead belongs to her father. It is significant in this respect that the way in which Lawrence restores Lydia's memory is through presenting her with one of her old toys that he has obtained from her father. In effect the gift causes her to regress to childhood, confirming Reid's assertion that she is altogether too young for romantic liaisons. (Like Reid, Lawrence does not appear to get the girl at the end of the film.)

The key difference between Lawrence and Reid, then, lies in their relation with Lydia's father. Lawrence acts on the father's behalf and confounds the false father; Reid acts alone and is defeated by Lydia's false father. The view of the world this suggests is, of course, a very paternalistic and authoritarian one. The effective man – Lawrence in this case – is the one who respects his seniors while the weak or troubled man is he who acts in isolation from or in defiance of the father. At the same time, the film is haunted by doubts as to the nature of this authority, with this most obviously manifested in a further doubling – that of Professor Menzel and Hendlmann, Lydia's two fathers. Late in the film, as part of a ruse to trick the woman claiming to be Hendlmann's wife into revealing the truth, Lawrence informs her that Hendlmann intends to marry Lydia. Her angry response shows that she has no problem believing this; the film itself is more circumspect about the question of whether Hendlmann desires Lydia although his possessiveness of his 'daughter' is clearly marked as sinister and unhealthy. In comparison with this, Professor Menzel, the true father, seems much more benign. However, even his relation to Lydia can be seen as having a possessive and potentially sexual dimension. 'It's Lydia, my Lydia', he exclaims on first seeing the portrait. He then shows Lawrence a photograph of his wife who turns out to be the spitting image of his daughter (the photo appears to be of Mai Zetterling herself). Lawrence's returning to him the woman who is the image of his lost wife, and Lawrence's own shying away from her as a sexual object, has an uneasy quality to it in this respect. It is as if Lydia is to replace the wife she so exactly resembles. The opposition set up by the film between the Professor, the sympathetically presented Austrian Jew, and Hendlmann, the villainous Nazi, is, in part at least, eroded by this sense of the possessiveness that characterises them both.

Portrait from Life offers a troubled view of male identity and authority, with much of this organised around the 'ownership' of Lydia and the question – never really resolved in the film itself – of whether she is best seen as a daughter, lover or wife. Lydia herself remains an enigma, the object of male investigation and struggle rather than a distinctive character in her own right. In this, *Portrait from Life* strikingly anticipates Hammer horror's portrayal of male identity in terms of an ambivalently presented paternalism. Having said this, one also needs to recognise that the film has a certain typicality about it so far as British cinema of the mid- to late 1940s is concerned. A range of films from this period show male characters as troubled, introspective, neurotic, with this often tied in with the end of the war and the difficulties for men in readjusting to civilian life. Examples include *Dead of Night* (1945), *A Matter of Life and Death* (1946), *The Captive Heart* (1946), *They Made Me a Fugitive* (1947) and Fisher's own *To the Public Danger*, although, even bearing this in mind, the particular 'Oedipal' slant taken by *Portrait from Life* is distinctive.

In other ways too, *Portrait from Life* points forward to Hammer. For one thing, it marked the first time that Fisher worked with cinematographer Jack Asher who would later be a major contributor to Hammer horror. Here Asher must be given credit for the noir-like qualities bestowed both upon the interior of the displaced person's camp and on the drinking den where a dying Reid is discovered. For another thing, *Portrait from Life* contains one sequence – Hendlmann's attack on an informer – that can reasonably be called 'Fisheresque' inasmuch as it anticipates in exact detail a number of sequences in Fisher's later films. The attack begins with Hendlmann in long shot, standing at the far end of a hut. He advances slowly upon the informer. There are some cuts to the informer's frightened face but in the set-up featuring Hendlmann the camera does not move until just before the attack begins. There is a static quality to the sequence which very effectively underlines the inexorability of Hendlmann's approach. This image – of a threatening figure moving forwards through a setting towards an immobile camera – shows up on several occasions in later films (in *Dracula*, *The Mummy*, *Dracula – Prince of Darkness*, etc.) to the extent that it can be seen as a kind of signature camera set-up, one which is presented here for the first time.

Confirming the inconsistency of Fisher's work in this period, the next project for Gainsborough, the portmanteau drama *Marry Me!* (1949), is much less successful. The portmanteau format – in which a film features several separate stories usually linked by a common theme or setting – would in the 1960s become a significant feature of the British horror cycle (although not one to which Fisher himself would ever contribute). Before then it had a variety of uses, as the cinematic approximation of the short story, for example (in *Dead of Night*, say, or films such as *Trio*, *Quartet* and *Encore* which adapted the short stories of W. Somerset Maugham), or as a way of presenting a cross-section of a class-divided British society without having to integrate the different sections into a cohesive whole. The mix of the tragic, the comic and the romantic found in *Marry Me!* is not particularly distinctive, however, and it would be hard to separate it out in terms of content or quality from other portmanteaux from the same period such as, for example, *Bond Street* (1948) or *Easy Money* (1948). Fisher's next, *The Astonished Heart*, was, as we have seen, something of a problem project and, as is the case with *Marry Me!*, it would be difficult to make any substantial claims for the film as a whole.

So Long at the Fair, Fisher's final film at Gainsborough (which, like *The Astonished Heart*, was co-directed with Antony Darnborough) is more interesting. The film's narrative deals with an English brother and sister (played by David Tomlinson – who had also appeared in the earlier *Marry Me!* – and Jean Simmons) who arrive in Paris for the 1889 Grand Exposition. The brother mysteriously vanishes from the hotel where they are staying and all the hotel staff deny that he ever existed. Only through enlisting the help of an English expatriate artist (played by Dirk Bogarde) does the sister discover that her brother has contracted the plague and has been spirited quietly away in order that the Exposition is not threatened. The film concludes with the sister reunited with the still desperately ill but slowly recovering brother.

David Pirie, an early champion of Fisher as auteur, has gone so far as to argue that *So Long at the Fair* 'demonstrates against all the odds that every major component of Fisher's world was already expressed on film before he even entered horror'.[17] In particular, he sees its stress on contagion as having a distinctly vampiric tone. 'So Long at the Fair could easily have been re-shot, sequence for sequence, as a vampire movie without making any difference to its basic mechanics, for the same dualistic structure pervades every frame. Presumably the film would then end with the staking of the brother to purify and purge the alien "infection" to which he has succumbed.'[18] The retrospective nature of this reading, the way in which it insistently views So Long at the Fair from the perspective of the later horror work, arguably obscures other interesting features of the film that are more to do with the immediate context of its production. However, if we adopt a prospective rather than retrospective position, then there is something to be said for Pirie's reading inasmuch as it successfully identifies the way in which Fisher in this period is acquiring cinematic experiences, both in terms of technique and dramatic content, that will be developed later on in his career. In the case of So Long at the Fair, the central brother/sister relationship clearly anticipates the Alan/Helen relationship in Dracula – Prince of Darkness (1966). One half of each couple – Johnny in So Long at the Fair, Helen in Dracula – Prince of Darkness – is prissy and distrustful of the foreign; subsequently they both become 'infected', Johnny by the plague, Helen by vampirism. Importantly, the differences between the two are just as striking as the similarities. For one thing, Johnny is something of a cipher; his main function is simply to disappear and once disappeared never to reappear. Even at the end of the film, we only see his sister Vicky looking at him, not Johnny himself. Helen, by way of a contrast, is a much more complex character and remains a compelling presence even, or particularly, after her infection.

Also significant is the fact that while Helen and her partner Alan are a relatively mature wife and husband, Johnny and Vicky are brother and sister whose immaturity is all too apparent in their dealings with the inhabitants of Paris. The English artist George seems to be there to facilitate Vicky's move away from her brother – on several occasions she is mistaken for her brother's wife – into a 'sexually mature' relationship. However, this relationship does not convince as a romantic one. Vicky is too concerned with her brother while George is just too diffident. There is an interesting moment in this respect where George, on hearing from Johnny that Vicky is his sister and not his wife, thoughtlessly remarks 'Bad luck'. The mutually embarrassed silence that follows is, one feels, the film's embarrassment as well; the idea that a brother might desire his sister is simply unthinkable, and the film retreats from the possibility as quickly as possible. Another director might well have explored some of the perversities apparent in this situation. (In fact, a few years later Otto Preminger would do precisely that with *Bunny Lake is Missing*, a thriller from 1965 centred upon a very curious brother–sister relationship). At this stage in his career, Fisher preferred instead to suppress such scandalous elements in order that a sense of English innocents abroad, threatened on all sides by deceptive foreigners, might be preserved. Certainly *So Long as the Fair* uses every means at its disposal – including menacing close-ups and sinister lighting – to incriminate the hotel staff after Johnny's disappearance.[19]

As was the case with *The Astonished Heart* and *Portrait from Life*, the visual style that characterises the later horror films is also becoming apparent, albeit sporadically. One thinks in particular of the moment where George, having discovered Johnny's walled-up hotel room, proceeds to smash a chair through one of the flimsy walls. Pirie overstates matters when he suggests that the 'smashing of the attractive exterior of the Parisian hotel effectively shatters the seductive veneer of Paris as surely as the stake entering the luscious female vampire in *Dracula* transforms her into a haggard old crone',[20] but certainly the sequence looks forward to the ways in which Dracula, the Mummy and various other monsters crash in and out of domestic households in Fisher's horror work.

So Long at the Fair was the last costume picture to be made by Gainsborough. The earlier costume melodramas from that studio had notoriously featured rampant and murderous aristocrats, wicked ladies with plunging necklines, and narratives driven by desire. In comparison, *So Long at the Fair* is a rather passionless affair. Significantly in this respect, the film's major act of transgression involves nothing more than throwing a chair at a wall.

There is something decidedly quotidian about this moment in its preference for the physical and the material over the more inexpressible, excessive passions that motivated earlier Gainsborough melodramas, and in this too *So Long at the Fair* can be seen as anticipating Fisher's later work. Of course, this is a retrospective point (it's hard to see Fisher's pre-horror work without being retrospective in some way), but it does seem that it is this quality, this stress on the physical, that also separates out *So Long at the Fair* from its melodramatic predecessors.[21] The space of the hotel is not a space amenable to desire; it is too decorous and refined for that. Instead all that it invites is an assault upon its fabric carried out by a diffident English artist who, so far as one can make out, does not even get the girl at the end of the film.

So Long at the Fair was not only the last Gainsborough melodrama but also one of the last films ever made by that company. Gainsborough closed in the early 1950s. Throughout the second half of the 1940s, when Terence Fisher was working there as a director, Gainsborough had never been a home for British cinema's 'name' directors. These – including David Lean, Michael Powell, Roy and John Boulting, Sidney Gilliat and Frank Launder – were all working elsewhere after the war (although Launder and Gilliat did work for Gainsborough during the war with, amongst others, *Millions Like Us* in 1943 and *Waterloo Road* in 1945). Fisher in the early 1950s certainly did not have a critical reputation even remotely comparable with any of the film-makers listed above; in fact, it would be fair to say that he hardly had a reputation at all. Already linked with the sort of lower-budget genre pieces that were unlikely to generate critical plaudits (although occasionally they did) or attract much notice from the industry itself, Fisher was not in a good position professionally when the crisis came at Rank. Accordingly, along with a number of other directors who had been working at Gainsborough in the mid-1940s – amongst them Leslie Arliss, Bernard Knowles, Arthur Crabtree and David MacDonald – his career took what appeared to be a distinct turn for the worse. In Fisher's case, this meant his working for the next few years in one of the least promising areas of British film production in this period – the low-budget support feature.

Fisher in support

The full supporting programme – with each major film accompanied by a shorter narrative film and a newsreel (and sometimes by live entertainment as well) – faded away as a cinema exhibition practice in the 1960s but throughout the 1950s it was a standard feature of British cinema-going. The British film industry responded by churning out a large number of 60–80 minute programme-fillers (over 300 in the 1950s), the majority of them crime thrillers.[22] These support features often used minor or fading American stars, the presence of whom was clearly intended to make the films in question more attractive not only to British audiences but to American ones as well (although, given the parochial nature of the sector of British production, international success was always going to be an unlikely prospect). Writing in 1982, film critic Tim Pulleine catches some of the flavour of this type of film, and especially its crime variant: 'anyone whose film-going memory is long enough will retain a jumbled impression of B-pictures which contrived to suggest that the streets of London were thronged by American reporters, private eyes and ex-servicemen, incarnated by such performers as Dane Clark and Wayne Morris, and apt at every reel-change to stumble upon a dead body in Belgravia'.[23]

Between *So Long at the Fair* (released in 1950) and *The Curse of Frankenstein* (released in 1957), Terence Fisher directed nineteen films, all of them support features. Thirteen of these were crime thrillers – namely *Home to Danger* (1951), *The Last Page* (1952), *Wings of Danger* (1952), *Mantrap* (1953), *Blood Orange* (1953), *Face the Music* (1954), *The Stranger Came Home* (1954), *Final Appointment* (1954), *Murder by Proxy* (1955), *The Flaw* (1955), *Stolen Assignment* (1955), *The Last Man to Hang?* (1956) and *Kill Me Tomorrow* (1957). The remainder included a motor-racing drama (*Mask of Dust*, 1954), a medical drama (*A Distant Trumpet*, 1952), a comedy (*Children Galore*, 1954) and three films which have often been classified as science fiction: *Stolen Face* (1952), *Four Sided Triangle* (1953) and *Spaceways* (1953). An evaluation of Fisher's work in this period would do well to come to terms first with the support or 'B' feature itself as a particular cinematic format, and particularly the 'B' crime film.

The 'B' movie, especially in its American variant, has often been presented by critics as an area of relative freedom for film-makers. Because of the low budgets involved in 'B' movies, it has been suggested, studios monitored the activities of the film-makers to a lesser extent than they did in the case of more expensive films. This way of thinking about Bs is frequently coupled with a sense that the American 'B' movie in particular has at certain points in film history offered a space for the expression (often covert) of unconventional or even socially critical ideas. While such an approach has been very productive in terms of the critical work it has generated, the picture it offers of certain film-makers transcending the constraints imposed by an industry conceived of as either philistine or unquestioningly supportive of society's dominant values can be seen as offering a rather romanticised view that does not take proper account of the economic realities of film production. As James Naremore, historian of film noir – a key genre in the positive evaluation of the 'B' movie – has pointed out, many of the classic films noir were actually too expensive to be Bs and in fact fell into an intermediate category between 'B' and 'A' productions (B+ perhaps).[24] Naremore provides a salutary reminder that industrial categories and classifications do not always match critical ways of dividing up and valuing films.

So far as the British 'B' movie is concerned, a more apt comparison would not be with, say, film noir but rather with the 'poverty row' productions of American studios such as Monogram or Republic, films which have rarely received the positive critical attention afforded the more expensive Bs. These British support films were usually made for £10,000–20,000 on three-week shooting schedules (although the Danziger brothers, prolific producers in this area, were reported to have ten-day shooting schedules). Production was often based in small studios where the technical resources were inferior to those offered by major studios such as Pinewood or Elstree. Camera movements were minimal – because of the time it took to organise such movements and the limited space available in the small studios – and, in comparison with more expensive films, considerably less time was spent in lighting the set. The outcome of this were films that were often visually static and talkative, with only intermittent bouts of action. Inasmuch as values and ideas were expressed, they tended to be utterly conventional ones. One critic's weary description of Fisher's 1952 film *Wings of Danger* can stand in this respect for this type of film generally: 'Thriller with a moral ending, in which the good people survive and the bad ones don't. In this, as in other ways, quite unremarkable.'[25]

Clearly this was an area of British cinema which offered minimal opportunities for a director to intervene into or manipulate a particular film in ways that could be seen as authorial. Moreover, the low budgets involved led to a lack of prestige which in turn meant that critics of the time devoted little attention to support features. Unlike other areas of low-budget production (1970s British exploitation cinema, for example), the films themselves are also not of the type to attract the attention of cultists: they are just too straight, both morally and aesthetically, to sustain 'alternative' or transgressive readings. Consequently, the British support feature of the 1950s remains a relatively unexplored aspect of British film production. Even auteurist accounts of Fisher (with the exception of Wheeler Winston Dixon) have tended to skip over this part of the career.

Some of the difficulties involved in finding signs of Fisher's 'authorship' in this support-feature work become apparent from an appraisal of his 1952 film *The Last Page*. Made for Hammer at Bray Studios, this crime thriller (as did most Hammer films of the period) featured American stars, in this case George Brent and Marguerite Chapman, alongside British character actors – Raymond Huntley, Peter Reynolds, Eleanor Summerfield, Harry Fowler and a young Diana Dors. Based on a James Hadley Chase play, the film's scenario lends itself, superficially at least, to being seen as 'Fisheresque'. Brent plays a respectable, happily married bookshop manager who, while working late one night, ends up kissing his assistant (played by Diana Dors). The kiss is quite out of character for both the manager and the fun-seeking but essentially decent assistant. The consequences of the kiss are disastrous, however. Dors' criminal boyfriend forces her to blackmail Brent; the blackmail escalates into something murderous with the accidental death of Brent's crippled wife and then the death of Dors at the hands of her boyfriend. Brent ends up on the run from the police, the main suspect for Dors' killing.

Implicit in the idea of a kiss that leads to murder is a theme we have already identified as being of some significance, albeit intermittently, in Fisher's work – that is, the dangerousness of desire, of succumbing to impulse. However, as is so often the case with these support features, the experience of actually watching the film offers less than the scenario promises. Given the limited resources at his disposal, Fisher has constructed an efficient entertainment but not one which makes much of what, on paper at least, is an intriguing idea. That *The Last Page* turns out to be dramatically rather insipid is partly to do with its workmanlike pacing and partly with a certain visual flatness. It has already been suggested that those moments in Fisher's work that might be seen as deriving from his input – Hendlmann's attack on the informer in *Portrait from Life*, the chair-throwing in *So Long at The Fair*, the banister shot from *The Astonished Heart* – are all dependent on a visual depth of field, on there being a considerable distance between the objects filmed and the camera. There are no moments of this kind in *The Last Page* simply, one presumes, because of the relatively small sets and the economy of the shooting schedule. This does not mean that the film is entirely bereft of interesting material – for instance, in a scene where the fugitive Brent hides out in a ruined church, the ruins themselves are effectively used to represent the state of his mind – but these tend to operate on the margins of what in the main is a decidedly prosaic drama.

One 1952 critic concluded his lukewarm review of *The Last Page* with the comment that it contained 'one exciting shot'.[26] Unfortunately the reviewer failed to specify which shot he was talking about, and I have been unable to identify it. However, in the other crime thrillers directed by Fisher in this period, one can occasionally locate – if one looks hard enough – isolated moments or shots which for this type of film are out of the ordinary. These often involve expressive camera movements; one thinks here in particular of some subjective camerawork in *Face the Music* and *Mantrap*. Clearly such glimmerings of distinctiveness and difference are insufficient to support even the most timorous of auteurist readings. At most they imply a film-maker who within an extremely constrained situation had the opportunity every now and then to try out an idea. Interestingly, these moments – the subjective shots mentioned above, the clever use of a mirror in *Mantrap* to create different planes of depth – are often associated with an attempt to open up and explore the limited space available to Fisher. While there are not enough of these moments here to affect the audience's perception (or the critic's perception for that matter) of the drama, the ability to make the most in visual terms of what were often very small sets would, in a more sustained and developed form, stand Fisher in very good stead with his later horror work.

What this suggests is that hunting for signs of distinctive direction or authorship in this area of cinema can be a futile activity. It is in the nature of these films – and especially the crime films which constitute their majority – to be repetitive and predictable. For all their concern with sensational crime and murder, they usually offer a low-intensity drama based on a certain familiarity and cosiness. In fact, the argument could be made that the best way to understand and indeed appreciate these films is cumulatively, through seeing lots of them (as British audiences of the 1950s would have seen lots of them). Only in this way, for one thing, does the quality of certain performers, especially those in support of the American stars, become apparent; for instance, Eleanor Summerfield, who appears in a number of these films (including four for Fisher) emerges from undeserved obscurity as an epitome of female sassiness. It does not follow that all these films are therefore exactly the same, however. In the case of Fisher, some of the work – notably *Face the Music* and *Final Appointment* – is more lively and entertaining than relentlessly tedious projects such as *Wings of Danger* or *Mantrap*. Yet one feels that there is actually not much to say about a film like *Face the Music* other than it is better paced than a film like *Wings of Danger*, with better performances and a more interesting setting.

Fisher directed six non-crime films between 1951 and 1956. Of these, the racing drama *Mask of Dust* is virtually indistinguishable from the crime films, with the racing scenes and the intrigue associated with them taking the place of criminal acts. The so-called science fiction drama *Spaceways* also turns out to be a kind of crime movie. Here the story revolves around the disappearance of a rocket scientist's wayward wife. Did he murder her and secrete her body in a rocket which he then launched into space? As it turns out, he is innocent; his wife has actually run away with her lover who, for good measure, is revealed as a spy working for a foreign power. *Spaceways* exhibits a notable lack of interest in scientific developments and their social implications. Instead it is far more concerned with the two romantic triangles it conjures up between, on the one hand, the scientist, his wife and her lover and, on the other, the scientist, his wife and a female scientist. In this respect it stands some distance from later British SF films such as *The Quatermass Experiment*, *Quatermass II* (and the television series upon which they were based) and *X – The Unknown* which do focus on more traditional SF themes and ideas.

I have not been able to view *A Distant Trumpet*, one of Fisher's other films from this period, but by all accounts it is an unimpressive drama dealing with the exploits of two brothers who become doctors, one in England and one in Africa. *Children Galore* is an altogether odder prospect. Ostensibly a comedy, it was produced by Grendon Films, a company which subsequently specialised in short films for children, although, ironically, the subject matter of *Children Galore* renders it rather unsuitable for a child audience. The film is set in a village where the lord and lady of the manor have decided to give a newly built house to the local married couple who have the largest number of grandchildren. An undignified competition ensues between local families as to whose offspring can produce the most children. The driving force behind this competition are the women in the families, and a linking together of female fecundity and female greed provides the film with much of its narrative drive. In one scene, this becomes quite grotesque as one of the women greedily consumes some mush-rooms she has picked earlier in the woods. Her face contorts into an exaggerated expression of satisfaction as she eats. The next scene is the woman's funeral; the mushrooms were poisonous and her greed has led to her death. The most remarkable thing about this scene is that it is played, albeit unsuccessfully, for laughs (broad comedy was never Fisher's strong suit). In fact, there is an uncertainty of tone about the film as a whole which renders it a somewhat unsettling experience. Fisher's tendency to play things straight means that potential ironies – for instance, the new house so desired by various women is conspicuously less attractive than the cottages in which most of the characters already live – are lost.

Fisher's two remaining films from this period – *Stolen Face* and *Four Sided Triangle* – are also odd projects, albeit more successful and interesting ones than *Children Galore*. Like *Spaceways*, *Four Sided Triangle* is that rare beast, a pre-1956 British science fiction film. While it follows *Spaceways* in privileging romantic relationships over scientific investigations, it nevertheless embraces more thoroughly some of the ideas and conventions associated with the SF genre. *Stolen Face* is harder to classify; sometimes linked with SF and horror because of its subject matter – a surgeon operating on a woman to transform her into a replica of another woman – it is probably more accurate to think of it as a rather perverse romantic melodrama. Both films offer scenarios in which men seek to duplicate and/or create women, in *Four Sided Triangle* via a replication machine and in *Stolen Face* by surgery. Such a theme crops up in a number of SF/horror texts, notably Mary Shelley's 1818 novel *Frankenstein*, Villiers De L'Isle Adam's 1886 novel *The Future Eve* and films ranging from the sublime – *The Bride of Frankenstein* (1935) and Fisher's own *Frankenstein Created Woman* (1967) – to the truly ridiculous – *Weird Science* (1985) and the unforgettable (no matter how hard you try) *Frankenhooker* (1990).

A comparison between *The Future Eve* and Fisher's two films is particularly instructive, both for what it says about this theme generally and for what it reveals about Fisher's take on it in *Stolen Face* and *Four Sided Triangle*. Adam's novel tells of a man who has fallen in love with a woman in whom there appears to be a disparity between her goddess-like physical appearance and her vulgar and common character. As the ardent male lover says: 'I seriously think that this woman has strayed by mistake into the form of the goddess – that this body does not belong to her.'[27] A scientist friend offers to construct a robot replica of the woman that would be physically indistinguishable from the original but would have a more fitting character. (The book makes clear that for the men concerned this means more compliant and respectful of the male.) As one might expect, the experiment ends badly with the male lover, the woman and her robot replica killed in a fire. Even before this ultimate disaster has been reached, the reader has been made aware of the monstrousness of this male project, of the way in which it seeks to efface the reality of the woman and replace it with what in effect is an egotistical male fantasy. Accompanying this is a sense of the sheer impossibility of doing this; the experiment will fail if reality intrudes and destroys the fantasy but it will also fail if reality does not intrude because then all you will have is an inanimate fantasy. In *The Future Eve*, it turns out that the robot woman's vision, a key feature of her life-like qualities, has been provided not by the scientist but instead in some mysterious way by the spirit of a comatose woman (the plot is nothing if not convoluted); the robot woman's animation and her appeal is thereby bound up with her tantalising Otherness and the inability of men fully to understand or define her.

There is no evidence that Terence Fisher or anyone else involved in the production of either *Stolen Face* or *Four Sided Triangle* had read or even knew about *The Future Eve*. Instead this seems to be a case of Fisher and his collaborators tapping into the same broad cultural theme around which *The Future Eve* and other works had already been constructed – namely the disparity between the lived reality of the woman and male fantasies about and/or idealisations of her. Significantly, Fisher's two films provide a much less harsh version of this than that offered by *The Future Eve*, one which permits in both films an outcome that would have been unthinkable in Adam's novel – a happy ending. In line with this, both *Stolen Face* and *Four Sided Triangle* begin very differently from *The Future Eve*. In Adam's novel the hero laments that his perfect woman, the match for his desire, does not exist in reality whereas the equivalent male characters in Fisher's films actually meet their perfect women only to lose them to other men. In

Stolen Face, Philip Ritter (Paul Henreid) encounters and falls in love with concert pianist Alice (Lizabeth Scott), only subsequently to discover that she is already engaged, while in *Four Sided Triangle* Bill (Stephen Murray) loves Lena (Barbara Payton) although she is engaged to Bill's friend, Robin Grant (John Van Eyssen). Another important difference is that in *The Future Eve* the male lover and the scientist are separate characters; in Fisher's films, they are one and the same person – Ritter is a surgeon, Robin an inventor. The consequence of this is that having been denied their ideal love the men themselves will attempt via scientific or medical means to reconstruct the lost woman. Desire and scientific knowledge thereby become inextricably linked.

In *Stolen Face*, Ritter operates on Lily, a scarred, working-class ex-convict, to give her Alice's face and subsequent to this he marries her.[28] With its sense of science gone bad, this scenario has some obvious Frankenstein-like qualities about it. The way in which Ritter is introduced to us is interesting in this respect. We begin with a shot of Ritter's hand, then the camera pulls back to show him examining a small boy whom he has just cured of some unspecified condition. The boy's mother thanks Ritter profusely and indicates that she will pay the surgeon's fee as quickly as possible (although she is obviously not wealthy). After she and the boy have left, Ritter comments to a colleague: 'Why is it that the poor always worry about paying their bills while the rich have to be reminded?' As if to underline this distinction, Lady Harringay enters. An older woman clearly signalled as vain, she enquires about the possibility of having cosmetic surgery in preparation for her forthcoming marriage. Ritter advises against such surgery; apparently some previous work on her face has been botched by another surgeon to the extent that further surgery would almost inevitably fail. Lady Harringay, obviously unused to being denied in this way, leaves in high dudgeon. Then Ritter and his colleague travel to Holloway Women's Prison where, somewhat improbably, they operate regularly on scarred and deformed women in order to render them attractive and, apparently, reduce their criminality. Ritter is introduced to his next patient, the aforementioned Lily who was horribly scarred in the Blitz and has been a compulsive criminal ever since. The schematic division thus offered between the undeserving rich and the needful poor is reproduced in Fisher's later *The Revenge of Frankenstein* (1958), where the eponymous Baron moves freely between his upper-class society practice and the working-class free hospital. What is significant here is that while Fisher can be seen as taking forward some elements from *Stolen Face* (along with elements from his other pre-1956 films) and redeploying them within Hammer horror, in important respects *Stolen Face* is very different in terms of theme and tone from the horror to come.

Most notably, Fisher's Frankenstein is singularly lacking in regret for what he does whereas Ritter is made to see how wrong his actions are. Indeed, the little homily that he offers to Lady Harringay – 'Learn to live with yourself as you are' – is one from which he himself might have benefited in his comprehensive inability to deal with Alice's absence. In this, Ritter turns out to be much like the psychiatrist in *The Astonished Heart*. Both offer advice to their patients which they themselves seem incapable of following.

Having Alice's face does nothing to assuage Lily's criminal tendencies. She steals, mixes with fellow criminals and other low-lifes and resists Ritter's attempts – notably his taking her to the opera – to make her more 'cultured'. In her combination of angelic appearance and pathological character (one character describes her as psychopathic), she is a yet more extreme version of the woman in *The Future Eve* who because of her beauty attracts male desire but is unwilling or unable to live up to that desire's demands. In *Stolen Face*, the disparity is underlined by the fact that in Alice we have already encountered the 'perfect' woman. Eventually a drunken Lily falls to her death from a speeding train. We do not see her body in detail but it is clear that her new face has been destroyed. 'At least she'll never know what it is to go through life disfigured', remarks an onlooker. The true Lily has re-emerged and Ritter is free to go off with Alice (who, conveniently, has been abandoned by her fiancé).

Four Sided Triangle proceeds in a comparable manner. Bill wants Lena but cannot have her because she is engaged to Robin.

So Bill, like Ritter, decides to make a duplicate woman with the replicating machine invented by himself and Robin. An initially reluctant Lena agrees to co-operate, the replication takes place and Helen, the double of Lena, is born. Unfortunately, the experiment succeeds too well for Helen is so exact a copy of Lena that she too loves Robin rather than Bill. An ever-resourceful if increasingly desperate Bill then plans to erase Helen's memories, but during this procedure the machinery fails and both Helen and Bill are killed in the ensuing fire. Lena survives and is happily re-united with Robin. This restoration of the couple is made possible, ironically in a film about duplication, by the doubling not only of Lena and Helen but also of the two inventors, Robin and Bill. The problematic, troubling couple – Bill and Helen – can therefore be destroyed while the good and 'normal' couple – Lena and Robin – survive. (In this, the film is comparable with Fisher's *Dracula – Prince of Darkness*, another film containing two couples, one of whom is destroyed, the other permitted to survive.)

As is the case with those other pre-1956 Fisher films that are distinctive in some way or other, there appears to be a conservative tone to the proceedings here. A comment made by the old doctor in *Four Sided Triangle* might well stand for this aspect of the work generally: 'There is often less danger in the things we fear than in the things we desire.' Desire is threatening, sexuality is dangerous, and anyone 'infected' with desire – whether it be Bill in *Four Sided Triangle*, Ritter in *Stolen Face*, Duncan Reid in *Portrait from Life* or Chris in *The Astonished Heart* – will suffer because of it. Yet at the same time this fearful emotion of desire is also an object of considerable fascination for the films. One outcome of this is that both *Stolen Face* and *Four Sided Triangle* reveal and dwell upon some of the more disturbing aspects of male desire, and their conservative but also somewhat contrived conclusions do little to resolve issues raised elsewhere in the films.

In the case of *Four Sided Triangle*, for instance, the fact that Bill's desire for Lena leads to his attempt to erase Helen's memory, in effect to lobotomise her, arguably reflects back on Robin's desire for Lena. The dichotomy set up by the film, with the normal Robin/Lena relationship on one side and the deviant Bill/Helen relationship on the other, is undermined by the way in which the film stresses the similarity between the two men – men who are lifelong friends, both inventors, in certain respects almost inter-changeable. Similarly, the opposition in *Portrait from Life* between the strong David Lawrence and the weak Duncan Reid is haunted by the fact that they occupy a comparable position in relation to Hildegard/Lydia. If the splitting of masculinity here registers an attempt (usually unsuccessful) to deal with some anxiety relating to male identity, it also clearly demonstrates and constantly reminds us that there is a problem there in the first place. As indicated above, the double functions in this way as an ambiguous figure, both reassuring and threatening.

It follows that one should not simply write off these films as conservative and/or reactionary (as sometimes Fisher's work has been written off) simply on the basis of either their conclusions or the moralistic 'messages' occasionally offered by them. What one needs instead is a sense of how these films' narratives operate as processes by which certain values are threatened, sometimes over-turned, sometimes restored or revised. The moral and ideological positions adopted by characters within films and by the films themselves are invariably unstable precisely because narrative demands change and instability. Each narrative will proceed via both its instigation and its management of a whole range of instabilities and uncertainties. In the case of Fisher's *Stolen Face* and *Four Sided Triangle* (along with earlier films such as *Portrait from Life* and *The Astonished Heart*), these instabilities and uncer-tainties relate to masculinity, and they are not dispelled at the films' conclusions. Anxiety is the keynote here, not a conservative reassurance. (I'm not suggesting that because of this these films should therefore be seen as 'progressive' in any way. Identifying films in such either/or terms, as either conservative or progressive, seems to me to be an overly simplistic exercise, one which takes precious little account of the ways in which films actually operate as narratives.)

Having said this, there is not much to distinguish either *Stolen Face* or *Four Sided Triangle* formally or in terms of production values from the other support features made by Fisher in this period. (*Four Sided Triangle* had a slightly larger budget than usual – £25,000 – to help, presumably, with the film's very modest special effects. The increased budget does not seem to have had any appreciable effect on the film generally.) Certainly in their respective subject matters, and their treatment of it, these films stand apart, but in other ways – in their pacing and their general ambience – they sink back into the mass. It follows that one should not over-value them simply in the interests of bolstering Fisher's status as an author-director. Ultimately these are modest achievements, not without interest and signs of directorial ability but at the same time not so striking as to merit attention as major works.

It is likely that an evaluation of Fisher's career made in 1956 would not have rated him particularly highly. Fisher himself would probably have emerged as a capable but undistinguished film-maker working in some of the less exciting and glamorous areas of British film production (including not only his support work but also the films at Highbury and Gainsborough). With the benefit of hindsight, such an evaluation can be challenged in certain respects. *To the Public Danger* and *Portrait from Life* deserve more attention than they have thus far achieved; *Portrait from Life*'s critical obscurity is especially undeserved. One can also detect an intermittently expressed but definitely present set of thematic concerns to do with masculinity as well as a certain facility with the camera (although again this is not constant throughout Fisher's pre-horror work).

However, the most important features of Fisher's career at this stage are less to do with either the content or form of his films and more to do with where he actually was in the industry. For one thing, he had by the mid-1950s acquired substantial experience of low-budget film production. For another, from 1951 onwards he had formed an association with a small, independent production company called Hammer Films. Neither of these factors would have seemed that important at the time, but they were about to make Fisher a key player in one of the more sensational developments in post-war British film history.

Notes

1 Brian McFarlane, *An Autobiography of British Cinema* (London, Methuen), 1997, p. 332.

2 See David Pirie, *A Heritage of Horror: The English Gothic Cinema 1946–1972* (London, Gordon Fraser), 1973, pp. 61–3 for a detailed discussion of this sequence.

3 Andrew Sarris, 'Notes on the auteur theory in 1962', *Film Culture*, 27 (Winter 1962/63), p. 8.

4 Pauline Kael, 'Circles and Squares', in Gerald Mast and Marshall Cohen (eds), *Film Theory and Criticism*, 2nd edition (Oxford, Oxford University Press), 1979, p. 674.

5 For details about *Tonight at 8.30*, see Raymond Mander and Joe Mitchenson, *Theatrical Companion to Coward* (London, Rockliff), 1957, pp. 192–240.

6 See Graham Payn and Sheridan Morley (eds), *The Noel Coward Diaries* (London, Weidenfeld & Nicolson), 1982, p. 129 and Michael Redgrave, *In My Mind's Eye: An Autobiography* (London, Weidenfeld & Nicolson), 1983, pp. 186–7.

7 Peter Wollen, *Signs and Meanings in the Cinema*, 3rd edition (London, Secker & Warburg), 1972, p. 104.

8 Payn and Morley (eds), *The Noel Coward Diaries*, p. 129. To make matters yet more complicated, extra footage had to be shot to make *The Astonished Heart* acceptable to the American censor. According to film historian Anthony Slide, most of this new material involved some of the film's minor characters expressing a censorious disapproval of the adulterous affair. The new version of the film was prepared by Antony Darnborough; it is not clear whether Fisher was involved. See Anthony Slide, *Banned in the USA: British Films in the United States and Their Censorship, 1933–1960* (London, I. B. Tauris), 1998, pp. 31–3. The version of *The Astonished Heart* that occasionally shows up on British television is the British release version. So far as I am aware, the American release version has never been shown in Britain.

9 Andy Medhurst, 'That special thrill: *Brief Encounter*, homosexuality and authorship', *Screen*, 32:2 (Summer 1991), p. 199.

10 For more on Highbury, see Geoffrey MacNab, *J. Arthur Rank and the British Film Industry* (London, Routledge), 1993, pp. 146–8. For a brief account of some of the 'horrors' of working at Highbury during the war, see Adrian Brunel, *Nice Work: 30 Years in British Films* (London, Forbes Robertson), 1949, pp. 192–3.

11 This type of film was not peculiar to British cinema as the existence of American features such as *The Cat and the Canary* (1927, 1939, 1979) and *The Ghost Breakers* (1940), amongst others, testifies.

12 *Monthly Film Bulletin*, 15:176 (August 1948), p. 109.

13 MacNab, *J. Arthur Rank*, p. 147.

14 'The broadcast of *To the Public Danger* was followed by a renewed avalanche of fan mail – but also a considerable number of hate letters from the lunatic fringe of the motoring lobby, who saw the play as a hysterical blast against

their god-given right to drive how they liked, and as fast as they wanted.' Nigel Jones, *Through A Glass Darkly: The Life of Patrick Hamilton* (London, Abacus), 1993, p. 221.

15 Wheeler Winston Dixon, *The Charm of Evil: The Life and Films of Terence Fisher* (Metuchen, NJ and London, Scarecrow Press), 1991, p. 26.

16 Sigmund Freud, 'The Uncanny', in *The Penguin Freud Library – Volume 14: Art and Literature* (Harmondsworth, Penguin), 1990, pp. 335–76.

17 Pirie, *A Heritage of Horror*, p. 53.

18 *Ibid.*, p. 55.

19 For more on the film's xenophobia, see Pam Cook, *Fashioning the Nation: Costume and Identity in British Cinema* (London, BFI), 1996, pp. 110–14.

20 Pirie, *A Heritage of Horror*, p. 55.

21 The passivity of Vicky throughout much of this – after her brother's disappearance, she spends most of her time asking men to help her – also distinguishes her from the more assertive heroines found elsewhere in Gainsborough melodrama.

22 It is difficult to ascertain the exact number of such productions, mainly because it is sometimes hard to distinguish between support features and co-features. The economic distinction is clear enough – support features received a flat fee while co-features received a percentage of the box-office take. In addition, co-features tended to be longer in length and cost more money to make. However, running lengths and budgets are not always a reliable indicator of status in the market, and certain films could move from one category to another on the basis of business negotiations and/or box-office success. For an interesting short account of this sector of British film production, see Brian McFarlane, *Lance Comfort* (Manchester, Manchester University Press), 1999, pp. 118–25.

23 Tim Pulleine, 'Hollywood's baby brother? – British films of the fifties', *Films and Filming*, 339 (December 1982), p. 22.

24 James Naremore, *More than Night: Film Noir in its Contexts* (Berkeley, University of California Press), 1998, pp. 136–66.

25 *Monthly Film Bulletin*, 19:222 (July 1952), p. 98.

26 *Monthly Film Bulletin*, 19:221 (June 1952), p. 80.

27 Villiers De L'Isle Adam, 'The future Eve', in Peter Haining (ed.), *The Frankenstein Collection* (London, Artus Books), 1994, p. 95.

28 Incidentally, the idea of a surgeon 'curing' scarred women recurs in a more fetishistic form in *Circus of Horrors* (1960), one of the more lurid of British horror films, and also shows up in Terence Fisher's own *Frankenstein Created Woman* (1967).

1 Nan (Susan Shaw) and her dull boyfriend Fred (Barry Letts) in *To the Public Danger*

2 Margaret Leighton and Noel Coward as doomed lovers in *The Astonished Heart*

3 *Home to Danger*: a characteristic moment from one of Fisher's earliest support features

4 William Sylvester throws a punch in *The Stranger Came Home*, one of Fisher's 1950s thrillers for Hammer

5 Trade advertisement for Hammer's *Blood Orange*, making clear that 'It's a British Production'

6 *The Four Sided Triangle*: Hammer advertising hyperbole at work

7 Lois Maxwell is threatened by George Coulouris in *Kill Me Tomorrow*, Fisher's last thriller

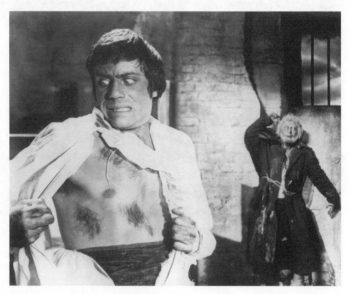

8 *Curse of the Werewolf*: Leon (Oliver Reed) on the turn as a worried Michael Ripper looks on

9 *Dracula – Prince of Darkness*: the vampiric Helen (Barbara Shelley)

10 *Dracula – Prince of Darkness*: the controversial staking of Helen – Father Sandor (Andrew Keir) wields the stake

11 Dennis Price acts villainous in *The Earth Dies Screaming*

12 *Night of the Big Heat*: production still of Patrick Allen and Sarah Lawson

13 *Frankenstein Created Woman*: Christina (Susan Denberg) as 'good'/weak/ scarred daughter

14 *Frankenstein Created Woman*: Christina resurrected as a murderous and seductive blonde

15 *Frankenstein Created Woman*: Cushing's Frankenstein at his most benign

The horror man: 1957–62

3

> I like period, legend, and allegory because they take you out of your personal present-day experience. After all, let's face the fact: this is entertainment. And entertainment is escapism ... Period vampire stories – even Frankenstein – are fairy tales. It is fantasy – grim fantasy, and grim fairy tale. That is a pun. But it's a good pun, because Grimm wasn't a gentle storyteller, was he? (Terence Fisher)[1]

Fisher and Hammer

It is not unreasonable to think of *The Curse of Frankenstein* as representing Terence Fisher's date with destiny. This enormously successful Hammer film, released in May 1957, both inaugurated the British horror boom and established Fisher as a film-maker whose name was known to critics, if only as someone who special-ised in the despised horror genre. After *The Curse of Frankenstein*, Fisher became primarily a horror director. Of his twenty-two post-*Curse* films, fifteen were period horror films and all but one of the remainder contained horror-like qualities or related elements of fantasy. For example, *Sherlock Holmes and the Deadly Necklace*, a film co-directed by Fisher in Germany in 1962, owed a clear debt to Fisher's 1959 Hammer film *The Hound of the Baskervilles* (a debt underlined by the presence of Hammer star Christopher Lee in both), *The Stranglers of Bombay* (1959), ostensibly a historical drama, functioned more as a gothic melodrama, while *The Horror of it All* (1964) was a horror-comedy. Then there were three science fiction invasion films – *The Earth Dies Screaming* (1964), *Island of Terror* (1966) and *Night of the Big Heat* (1967). In fact, Fisher's only 'wayward' project in the second half of his directorial career was the Robin Hood film *Sword of Sherwood Forest* (1960) which in the context of the horror boom seemed a nostalgic throwback to more innocent times.

It is also significant that of these twenty-two films, seventeen were made for Hammer, a company with which Fisher's fortunes would become closely tied. From *The Curse of Frankenstein* in 1957 to *The Phantom of the Opera* in 1962 – the years covered by this chapter – Fisher worked exclusively as a director for Hammer. If one discounts Hammer's *The Terror of the Tongs* (1961 – a Fu Manchu-like melodrama with some distant affinities with the Hammer horror mainstream), Fisher was actually responsible for all of Hammer's costume horror films in the 1957–1962 period. Later, from 1962 onwards, Fisher's relationship with Hammer would become more sporadic, but during Hammer's initial burst of horror-related activity, Fisher was, even by his standards, astonishingly prolific on behalf of the company. Between November 1956 – when *The Curse of Frankenstein* went into production – and the end of 1960, Fisher completed eleven feature films. In some cases, only a few days separated the end of principal photography on one film and the beginning of principal photography on another; so, to give two examples, *Dracula* finished shooting on 3 January 1958 and *The Revenge of Frankenstein* began on 6 January 1958, *The Two Faces of Dr Jekyll* ended on 22 January 1960 and *The Brides of Dracula* started on 26 January 1960.[2]

Such prolificity is only possible within an efficient and stable production context where roles and responsibilities are clearly defined. This is precisely what Hammer offered at this time. Not only had its pre-1957 production of support features already given it considerable experience of turning round films quickly on small budgets and with limited resources; Hammer was also able to offer a continuity in terms of location – it had been based at Bray Studios since 1951 and would stay there until 1966 – and personnel. So far as the latter was concerned, it was not only Fisher working extensively on horror productions between 1957 and 1962. In this period, Michael Carreras and Anthony Hinds (grandson and son respectively of Hammer's two founders, Enrique Carreras and Will Hinds) produced or executive-produced all of Hammer's horrors, Jimmy Sangster wrote six (and Anthony Hinds a further two under the pseudonym John Elder while also making an uncredited contribution to *The Brides of Dracula*), cinematographer Jack Asher photographed eight and production designer Bernard Robinson and supervising editor James Needs each worked on eleven. Peter Cushing and Christopher Lee, the two actors most associated with Hammer, were also busy; they each appeared in six Fisher-directed horror films (and Cushing also showed up in *Sword of Sherwood Forest*).

It is clear from this that throughout the first 'movement' of Hammer horror, from 1957 to 1962, Fisher was part of an established team, and the films he directed are not really understandable without reference to that team. As was noted in Chapter 1, any realistic account of Fisher's contribution to Hammer horror needs to be aware of the collaborative contexts within which he was working and should avoid giving him credit for elements in particular films which were manifestly the work of others. This inevitably means focusing on the staging of the horror dramas – their mise-en-scene – as the main area in which Fisher intervened into the production process (although even here giving due credit to cinematographer Jack Asher and production designer Bernard Robinson). Chapter 2's account of a scene from *The Astonished Heart* has already pointed out some of the difficulties involved in assigning a particular feature of a film to any individual in the absence of reliable and detailed information about the film's production. Having said this, there is a lot more information available about the production set-up at Hammer than there is material relating to Fisher's earlier work, and it is therefore possible to gain a clearer picture of what Fisher's role actually was at Hammer (as opposed to the somewhat murky circumstances of *The Astonished Heart*'s production) and consequently easier to provide a more measured assessment of his contribution and influence.[3]

Bearing this in mind, there is a strong case to be made for Fisher being a very major contributor to Hammer horror in the formative 1957–62 period. In large part, the distinctiveness of these films can be related to his treatment and presentation of material – scripts, production designs, casts – usually given to him, without much notice, by others. Fisher was not responsible for initiating any of these films, none of them were 'personal' projects, and there is no evidence that he (or, for that matter, anyone else at Hammer) even wanted to be a horror specialist. Yet at this particular moment late on in his career – let us not forget that Fisher was fifty-three when *The Curse of Frankenstein*, his first major success, was released – he at last found a subject that defined him as a film-maker and which he himself helped to define for British cinema.

Gothic beginnings

On their British release, *The Curse of Frankenstein* (released in May 1957) and *Dracula* (released in May 1958) garnered some extremely hostile reviews. C. A. Lejeune, the noted *Observer* film critic, thundered 'Without any hesitation I should rank *The Curse of Frankenstein* among the half-dozen most repulsive films I have encountered in the course of some 10,000 miles of film reviewing',[4] while Campbell Dixon at *The Daily Telegraph* suggested that a new censor certificate was needed for this type of film: '"SO" perhaps; for Sadists Only.'[5] However, the reviews for the early Hammer horrors were not universally hostile, and these films tended to be greeted as much with patronising amusement, bemusement and occasional praise as they were with outright condemnation.[6] What does link together many of these critical responses is a shared sense that the Hammer horror film represented something new, new in terms of both British cinema and horror cinema.

There is no reason to suppose that what was new and unsettling for the critics was not also going to be new and unsettling for the film-makers as well. So far as Fisher's career was concerned, *The Curse of Frankenstein* saw him breaking new ground in several ways. It was his first colour film, his first horror film, and also his first period costume drama since *Colonel Bogey*, his 1947 directorial debut. Much the same could be said for the rest of the Hammer team working on the film; and this lack of experience in the horror genre, along with the absence of any up-to-date examples to draw upon (in the post-war years, period horror films were few and far between until Hammer came along) might help to explain the uncertainty of tone that characterises *The Curse of Frankenstein* as well as some of the stiltedness of Fisher's direction as he struggles to come to terms with such unfamiliar material.

David Pirie has argued that 'Fisher is not essentially an expressionist film-maker ... His solemn, almost pedantic, style is that of the nineteenth-century storyteller; anything flashier or less solid would be unsuited to his material.'[7] It is true that in comparison with the baroque excesses and extravagant camera-work of James Whale's *The Bride of Frankenstein* (1935) or the 1960s horror films of American director Roger Corman and Italian directors Mario Bava and Riccardo Freda, Fisher's work seemed more sober and restrained. However, from the very beginning of Fisher's career in horror, this apparent sobriety was punctuated by moments and sequences that could in certain instances reasonably be described as expressive and which generally were all the more effective (and sometimes shocking) for the way they stood out against a relatively solid background. Perhaps the most striking example of this from *The Curse of Frankenstein* is the introduction of the Creature (played, of course, by Christopher Lee). In James Whale's 'classic' 1931 version of *Frankenstein*, the Monster's introduction is slow, with Boris Karloff shuffling backwards into a room and slowly turning to face the camera.[8] By way of a contrast, this introduction in *The Curse of Frankenstein* has an unnerving rapidity about it. Victor Frankenstein (Peter Cushing) throws open the laboratory door and finds his bandaged creation standing before him. We then have a *very* fast camera track towards the Creature as he pulls away bandages to reveal his horribly scarred face. There is nothing subtle about this camera movement; not for Fisher the atmospheric built-up offered by James Whale. Instead Fisher's sole intention here seems to be to shock the audience. It is hard to think of any comparable moment in British cinema of the 1940s and 1950s. In a way, this 'shock' effect is new for the horror genre as well, anticipating as it does the greater stress on shock scenes in horror from *Psycho* (1960) onwards.[9]

Elsewhere in the film Fisher tends to keep the camera at a distance, tracking laterally but rarely moving forwards. Sometimes this distance, and an attendant refusal to make rhetorical camera movements, is used very effectively. One thinks here in particular of two moments from the aged Professor Bernstein's visit to Frankenstein's castle. It has already been established that the Baron is searching for a brain for his Creature, and when Elizabeth, the Baron's fiancée, describes Bernstein as 'the greatest brain in Europe', Victor's surreptitious glance at the Professor's head speaks volumes. Bernstein and Frankenstein are framed here in medium shot sitting next to each other; any cutting in to a close-up of Frankenstein's look would have been too obtrusive, pushing the detail down our throats rather than allowing us to notice it ourselves. Similarly, a few minutes later, when the Baron shows the Professor a painting of what he describes as 'one of the early operations', it is clear even from a distance that in fact it is Rembrandt's famous 'The Anatomy Lesson' (not that Bernstein notices; as he inspects the painting, Victor pushes him off the balcony to his death). Providing a close-up of the painting would again underline the point too much, transforming a sly, unobtrusive joke into a clumsy bit of irony. This reticence carries over into some of the film's gorier moments: the smear of blood on Frankenstein's coat, the various operations with all their details hidden below the bottom frame-line (although, of course, the latter is also for censorship reasons). In all these cases, one has the sense that the positioning of the camera in relation to the drama has been thought out by Fisher, that it is part of a considered aesthetic. It might also be argued that much of the offence caused to critics by this film lies not in the amount of gore on show but instead in Fisher's apparently casual treatment of it.

Other sections of *The Curse of Frankenstein* are less successful, however. In the first half of the film especially, we are offered not only some rather unwieldy exposition but also lengthy conversation scenes mainly played out in the castle drawing room. These not terribly interesting scenes are filmed in a not terribly interesting manner, with an over-reliance on master shots that present us with flat tableaux within which various characters walk up and down while speaking their lines. This is 'theatrical' film-making in the most negative sense of the term, and, given the fluidity of mise-en-scene apparent in Fisher's earlier work, it is surprising to find it here.

One can only speculate as to the reasons behind the uneven-ness of the film. A possible reason for an over-reliance on static master shots could have been the expense of lighting multiple camera set-ups when filming in colour on a low budget (and with a director of photography – Jack Asher – known in the industry for his perfectionism). Another problem seems to lie with a screen-play which does not establish a consistent attitude to Frankenstein himself. Most Frankenstein films, both those produced at Hammer and elsewhere, tend to present Frankenstein as an ambiguous figure, part Promethean hero, part anti-social villain. However, in Sangster's screenplay, Hammer's version of this ambiguity has not been fully worked out, with this most apparent in an uncertainty over how to deal with those normative values that are challenged by Frankenstein's activities. The main normative and judgemental voice is provided by Paul Krempe, initially the Baron's tutor, then his accomplice and finally his antagonist. Unlike Elizabeth and Professor Bernstein – both of whom are completely ignorant of Frankenstein's questionable behaviour – Krempe is in a position to comment knowledgeably upon what Frankenstein is attempting to do. He is obviously a crucial character but it is never clear how we are meant to respond to him. He closely resembles the moralising types who show up in 1930s horror films and issue warnings about the moral and social consequences of the scientist's experiments, warnings which in 1930s horror usually turn out to be justified (although the audience has a lot of fun watching the rogue scientist at work). Yet in *The Curse of Frankenstein*, there is something vaguely irritating and distasteful about Krempe and the manner in which he constantly criticises Frankenstein but refuses to do anything about this; at the same time, he is never condemned outright by the film. This uncertain treatment becomes most apparent at the film's conclusion when Krempe visits

Frankenstein in prison on the eve of the Baron's execution. As the Baron begs his help, Krempe, his expression impassive, looks away from him and then leaves. Given that Krempe says very little in this scene, it is unclear why he visits the Baron. Is he a representative of morality here, or is there some furtive pleasure for him in seeing his enemy done in? (It is interesting in this respect – and provides Krempe with a clear motivation for not helping Frankenstein – that in the next scene we see him going away with Elizabeth, the woman with whom he is obviously in love and whom he can now take from his rival, the Baron. However, Fisher does not make anything of this.) The outcome of this is that when Frankenstein finally walks to the guillotine at the film's conclusion, we are left uncertain as to how *The Curse of Frankenstein* wants us to value its main character.

No such questions remain unanswered in Fisher's next film for Hammer, *Dracula*, and if there are any ambiguities (and there are a few) one feels that they have been consciously placed there by the film-makers. The move from *The Curse of Frankenstein* to *Dracula* turns out to be a move from a promising but flawed project to an extraordinarily accomplished piece of cinema, with this accomplishment registering in all sorts of different ways. Jimmy Sangster's screenplay is sharp and economical, Jack Asher's photography is splendidly atmospheric and Bernard Robinson's sets convey a sense of space far more effectively than did the rather cramped sets for *The Curse of Frankenstein*.[10] Most of all, Fisher's direction is superb; his camerawork and staging are elegant, and there is not a stilted or awkward camera set-up to be found anywhere in the film.

This startling transformation is apparent in *Dracula*'s opening sequence. To the accompaniment of James Bernard's strident score (surely one of the best ever written for a horror film), the camera tracks past a statue of what appears to be a bird of prey outside Dracula's castle and moves purposefully towards a cellar door. There is then a fade to the cellar interior; the camera continues moving forward towards a tomb, eventually closing in on the tomb's name plate – DRACULA. Suddenly the music stops and blood spatters on to the name plate. Fade to black. As Gregory

Waller has noted, this sequence 'remains effective primarily because ... it serves no obvious narrative purpose'.[11] Questions are raised here that the film subsequently does not even attempt to answer. Whose blood is this? How does the blood get on to the name plate when the tracking shot has just shown that the cellar is empty? In avoiding the wordy and laborious exposition of *The Curse of Frankenstein*, this sequence gives us instead a sense that the narrative is already under way before the film itself has properly started. At the same time, Fisher's camerawork immediately establishes a certain authority over the film's audience, for this is a camera that knows exactly where it is going and, whether we want it or not, it leads us into darkness and bloodshed.

This confident treatment of the story material is carried over into the following sequence which depicts Jonathan Harker's arrival at Castle Dracula.[12] Again lengthy exposition is avoided – Harker's voice-over diary entry quickly informs us that he is a librarian come to work in Dracula's library (although it is revealed shortly thereafter that he is in fact a vampire hunter out to destroy the Count). His entrance into the castle's main hall provides Fisher with a further opportunity for some bravura camerawork; as Harker moves slowly from left to right, the camera, which is initially on the right filming diagonally across the set, tracks from right to left until it ends up filming diagonally across the set from its left side. We have three carefully co-ordinated camera movements here: Harker's lateral walk across the set, the camera's lateral track in the opposite direction, and the camera's turning on its axis. It's a perfectly balanced shot – both Harker and the camera move at approximately the same speed – but it is also rather unsettling. In part, this is because the right-to-left track reminds us of, and in a sense is a reflection of or reply to, the sinister left to right track with which *Dracula* begins. There is also a certain tension set up in the shot between the different movements, with the camera tracking in an opposing direction to Harker and having to twist to keep him in the picture. Both elegant and disturbing, the shot is all the more remarkable for being so unobtrusive and economical; there is nothing remotely as good in *The Curse of Frankenstein* (or, for that matter, in any of Fisher's previous films).[13]

The clarity of Fisher's direction is aided by the screenplay's aggressive shortening of the *Dracula* narrative. The entire film takes place in or near Transylvania (unlike the original novel and the 1931 film, both of which move from Transylvania to England).[14] Not only does it open with Harker already fully knowledgeable about vampires; its Carlstadt section begins with Lucy already under the thrall of Dracula. In this urgent rush through the story, there is simply no time for the meandering dialogue scenes one finds in parts of *The Curse of Frankenstein*. The screenplay's treatment of its characters is also more confident, and introduces an element that would become important in many subsequent Hammer horrors – namely a clear division between strong, knowledgeable older men (here Peter Cushing's Van Helsing and Christopher Lee's Count Dracula) and weak younger men in need of guidance (here Jonathan Harker and Arthur Holmwood). The women, meanwhile, are defined entirely in terms of their relation to men: both Lucy and Mina become the focus of the struggle between Van Helsing and Dracula but have little to do other than die (Lucy) or be rescued (Mina).

It has to be said that Fisher was not solely or even mainly responsible for initiating any of this. It was presented to him by screenwriter Sangster (and, more indirectly, by Bram Stoker's novel). However, Fisher was largely responsible for developing and organising the presentation of this theme, and a particular strength turned out to be his ability to establish via visual means the authority and power of Dracula and Van Helsing. This is primarily done by showing how both these figures dominate and control space. One thinks here of Dracula's habit of appearing apparently from nowhere, from his first appearance in the film – when Harker looks up to find Dracula already standing at the top of the stairs in Castle Dracula – to his subsequent appearances at Lucy's bedroom window and in the hallway of the Holmwood house. In each case we do not see him arrive; he is just there. The film's opening sequence – in a cellar that is apparently empty but where the spattering of blood betrays the vampire's unseen presence – also suggests an uncanny control over off-screen space. At certain moments in the film, Van Helsing exerts a similar control, most strikingly in the scene where the vampiric Lucy approaches her hapless brother Arthur. Here Helsing's hand clutching a crucifix is suddenly thrust in from the side of the frame, effectively separating brother and sister. Given that for this to work in reality, Van Helsing would have had to walk right up to Arthur and Lucy without either of them noticing him, he too emerges from this, momentarily at least, as a quasi-supernatural presence.

Fisher's mise-en-scene also accentuates what had been a feature of the original novel but which had been marginalised in previous adaptations, namely the parallels between Dracula and Van Helsing, both of them paternalistic figures, one bad and the other good.[15] This is most apparent at the end of the scene in which Van Helsing has been reciting 'research on vampires' into a recording machine; as he makes his final comments about Dracula – 'He must be found and destroyed' – he is shown in close-up. There follows an unexpected cut to Dracula, also in close-up and compositionally occupying the same space as was previously occupied by Van Helsing. This juxtaposition – which was clearly formed during shooting by a director with an editor's experience – both highlights the absolute division between Van Helsing's rationality and modernity (as symbolised by the recording machine) and Dracula's world of desire, and at the same time undermines this division by stressing the similarity between these two figures. This doubling of authoritative males – one good, one evil – in a mutually defining relationship also features in some of Fisher's most distinctive later films, notably *Dracula – Prince of Darkness* (1966) and *The Devil Rides Out* (1968). As was discussed in Chapter 2, a doubling relationship between men can be found in some of Fisher's earlier pre-horror work – most obviously in *Portrait from Life* (1948) and *Four Sided Triangle* (1953). However, while these pre-horror doublings were associated with male anxiety and neurosis, the Dracula/Van Helsing doubling seems to confirm male authority, with the bad authority figure destroyed by the good authority figure but the authority they both embody left intact and unquestioned at the end of the film.

One of the conditions of the privileging of these powerful

authority figures is having weak men against whom they can be defined. In Fisher's *Dracula*, this weakness is represented by Jonathan Harker and Arthur Holmwood. As a knowledgeable vampire hunter, Harker turns out to be astonishingly ineffective. Even when he has Dracula at his mercy, he chooses to stake the less dangerous female vampire first, thereby permitting Dracula to escape. Arthur Holmwood is also, initially at least, something of a wimp. Refusing at first to accept the existence of the vampire, his subsequent refusal to allow the vampiric Lucy to be used as bait for Dracula results in his own wife then being threatened by the vampire. Only when he accepts Van Helsing's authority and agrees to do everything he is told is his wife then saved from Dracula (a rescue in which he himself only plays a marginal part).

As was the case with his portrayal of Van Helsing's and Dracula's power, Fisher conveys Harker's and Holmwood's weakness in an economical but effective manner, with this most evident at moments of maximum disempowerment (this to the extent that *Dracula* can reasonably be seen in terms of a movement between images of power and images of powerlessness). For Harker, this occurs when he is trapped in Dracula's tomb; as he drops the stake he is holding and stares helplessly at the Count, he is shot from above, the high angle accentuating his child-like helplessness.[16] Holmwood's maximal disempowerment occurs during his witnessing of Van Helsing's staking of Lucy. When the stake is hammered down, there is a cut to Holmwood clutching at his own chest (just as a few minutes earlier he had touched his own forehead after seeing Van Helsing burn the mark of the crucifix on to Lucy's forehead), his identification with the 'feminine' here stressed precisely when Van Helsing's masculinity is at its most unyielding and powerful.

This lack of authority carries over into Harker's and Holmwood's relations with women. From the beginning, Harker is helpless prey to the female vampire, and his attempt to reinstate his authority by staking her rather than Dracula ultimately leads to his own death. While we never see Harker (diffidently played by John van Eyssen) together with his fiancée Lucy, it is hard to imagine that he could ever have inspired the sexual passion Lucy clearly feels for Dracula (and which is beautifully conveyed by Fisher via an image of leaves shifting in the breeze as Lucy awaits the Count's nocturnal visit). Similarly, Arthur's relationship with his wife Mina is a curiously passionless one, and Mina's only sexual response derives, like Lucy, from her experience of Dracula.[17] As a number of critics have suggested (not only of the film but of the original novel as well), the most appalling thing that Dracula does to Victorian women is to make them sexual. In Fisher's *Dracula*, this is particularly explicit, with Dracula's attempt to replace the 'bride' staked by Harker involving the transformation of Lucy (and the threatened transformation of Mina) into a highly sexualised, predatory female.

So far as Fisher's film is concerned, such a threat clearly has to be contained, and the narrative concludes with an appropriately ferocious fight to the death between its two authority figures, Van Helsing and Dracula, within the walls of Castle Dracula. While the 1931 version of *Dracula* had been content to have the Count staked off-screen, Fisher – as he had done with *The Curse of Frankenstein* – stresses the physicality of the violence, with Dracula and Van Helsing frantically throwing themselves at each other. Perhaps the most distinctive moment in this sequence is also a highly 'physical' one: Van Helsing runs along a table, leaps off the end and pulls down some curtains, allowing light to pour in. He then forms a crucifix using two candlesticks and with this forces Dracula back into the sunlight where, before our eyes, the vampire turns to dust. It is well known that much of this – the Douglas Fairbanks-style leap off the table, the crucifix fashioned by candle-sticks – was actually Peter Cushing's idea, but the presentation of it is distinctly Fisher's.[18] An apparently simple and straightforward approach to filming the scene – with a master shot from the front interspersed with some closer shots of the two antagonists – turns out to involve a complex co-ordination of opposed movements (in a manner not dissimilar to the scene discussed above that depicts Harker's arrival in the castle). The table along which Van Helsing charges is angled so that it runs from the front left of the set towards the centre of the set's back wall, while the ray of light comes in from a point just above the far end of the table and is projected towards the front right of the set. Forming what in effect is the third side of a triangular composition – with the other two sides provided by the table and the ray of light – is the line along which Van Helsing will eventually force Dracula back into the light, a line which, like all the other compositional lines, runs at an angle to the main frontal camera position. There is a strong visual dynamism inherent in this set-up, with all the principal planes of movement and action at different angles in relation both to each other and to the camera, with this in turn unobtrusively emphasising the violent conflict that is the subject of the scene.

But the film does not end here. After a brief cutaway to Arthur reunited with Mina outside Castle Dracula, we return to Van Helsing as he walks away from an open window. There follows a shot of Dracula's ashes which are suddenly scattered by a breeze presumably coming from the open window. The end credits roll. It is an unsettling and ominous ending for a film which elsewhere has been so assertive and strident, and in its relative quietness there is perhaps a reminder of the ambiguous moment of silence near the film's beginning when blood from an unseen, never-to-be-known source is spattered on to Dracula's name plate. There is a sense in both instances – as there is elsewhere in the film – of counterpoint, of the juxtaposition of noise and silence, of the visible and the unseen, of certainty and doubt, which renders *Dracula* a considerably more subtle and complex work than has sometimes been supposed. In large part, this quality can be assigned to Fisher's contribution, with his perfectly judged pacing and his compositional skill proving a key factor in the formation of this most striking and accomplished of horror films.

Refinement of the formula

As principal photography on *The Revenge of Frankenstein* was concluding in March 1958, producer Anthony Hinds announced with typical Hammer hyperbole, 'World public demand for a Frankenstein sequel just could not go unheeded.'[19] In fact, the film that ensued was more of a refinement of the Hammer formula than a straight sequel, and one which offered a much more confident treatment of the Frankenstein story. The authority-subjection nexus around which Fisher's *Dracula* had been structured was carried over into *The Revenge of Frankenstein*, with a strict division observed between strong and weak men (and with women even more marginal than they had been in *Dracula*). However, here there was only one strong, authoritative male – Baron Frankenstein who, escaping the guillotine by having a priest executed in his place, is an altogether more sardonic figure than he ever was in *The Curse of Frankenstein*. One could hardly imagine this new model Baron begging for mercy as he does at the end of that film. His first appearance after his 'execution' typifies the revised, streamlined Frankenstein. 'Good evening, I am Baron Frankenstein', he announces to a grave-robber who promptly dies of shock; Frankenstein's response is a mildly bemused shrug. He has also become something of a dandy (as opposed to *The Curse of Frankenstein* where he was in the habit of accidentally smearing his clothes with blood); on several occasions Fisher shows him fastidiously placing a flower in his buttonhole. Within this clarifi-cation of the Frankenstein narrative, the rather irritating moral counter-force to the Baron that was provided by Paul Krempe in *The Curse of Frankenstein* has been removed entirely. Instead we are offered as the voice of 'social normality' the Medical Council, a motley collection of weak, pompous men who are presented by the film in unequivocally negative terms. *Revenge*'s other major innovation relates to its treatment of the monster – here the result of the transplanting of a cripple's brain into a new perfect body – who is shown as a humane figure rather than the snarling, scarred brute found in *The Curse of Frankenstein*.

In fact, it can be argued that *The Revenge of Frankenstein* contains two interrelated stories, the story of Frankenstein and his attempts to assert his authority both over other people and over the human body itself; and the story of Karl, the film's ostensible monster, and his suffering. Frankenstein's story is all about strength and the affirmation of the Baron's will; Karl's story deals instead with pain and vulnerability. The problem for Fisher in dealing with this material is that there is a certain contradiction built into it, for while our compassion for Karl's humanity compels us to view the Baron's indifference to suffering as cruel and inhuman, elsewhere we are invited to admire the Baron as a better sort of man than the weak, hypocritical members of the Medical Council. Fisher's response to this is to privilege neither Frankenstein nor Karl. Instead, via a mise-en-scene that avoids making rhetorical or moralising statements and which generally favours long and medium shots over close-ups, he presents a dispassionate account of both. So Frankenstein is given us in the positive – his challenge to the Medical Council's hypocrisy, his transgressive movement between his 'society' clinic and the poor hospital – and the negative – the fact that he sees his poor patients merely as collections of body parts. As for Karl, while it is true that we are meant to empathise with his suffering, at the same time the regression of his body becomes increasingly disgusting. This is most obvious in the disturbing conclusion to what is an already disturbing scene – the fight between Karl and the brutal, drunken janitor in charge of Frankenstein's laboratory. After having been badly beaten by the janitor, Karl strangles his assailant. In what for Fisher was already becoming a characteristic transition from a scene of noisy violence to a moment of unsettling quietness, we are then shown Karl looking from the janitor's dead body to a monkey in a nearby cage. Earlier in the film we had learned that this monkey had become a cannibal after having a brain transplant operation similar to that administered to Karl. The implication of Karl's staring at the animal after his longing gaze at the janitor's body is obvious enough (although sufficiently novel in the 1950s for Fisher to underline it by showing us that Karl is drooling), and the expression of disgust that appears on Karl's face as he becomes aware of his cannibalistic urges is clearly intended to mirror our own disgust.

These two story elements are finally brought together in a characteristic Fisher set-piece – the unexpected arrival of Karl at a society ball also attended by Frankenstein. Just as the Baron is about to leave, we hear the crash of broken glass. A dying Karl lurches towards Frankenstein, crying out the Baron's name and thereby revealing his hitherto hidden identity to all those present.

Karl then drops dead in front of his 'creator'. This is all filmed in a remarkably similar way to an earlier Fisher scene, Hendlmann's attack on the informer in *Portrait from Life* (discussed in Chapter 2). In each, someone advances from the back of the set towards another person standing closer to the camera; a near immobile camera set-up shows the advancing figure's progress with occasional cutaways to the face of the person being approached. Staging movement dynamically in relation to the camera was one of Fisher's strong points, and the director himself has spoken of always seeking to situate the monster within a particular setting rather than presenting him as an isolated figure: 'I've always involved the monster in the frame, planted him in the décor ... I've never *isolated* the monster from the world around, or tried to avoid showing him.'[20] However, while the technique might be similar (and it shows up in various forms in a number of Fisher's horror films), the meaning of each scene is quite different. In the simple version found in *Portrait from Life*, the advancing figure is more powerful than and a threat to the other person. In the more complex *The Revenge of Frankenstein*, Karl, the advancing figure, is weaker than Frankenstein, the person towards whom he moves, and inasmuch as he presents a threat, it is a threat to the Baron's social standing rather than to his physical well-being. In terms of its function within the film, the scene both reiterates and brings to a head the more pervasive ambiguity around the status of Frankenstein. On one level, we recognise the need for the Baron to be stopped, and his principal victim calling out his name effectively puts an end to his career. Yet the ball guests to whom Karl reveals Frankenstein's identity are hardly presented as a source of meaningful moral judgement.

Subsequently, the Baron is attacked and mortally wounded by his vengeful patients from the poor hospital. His faithful assistant then transplants his brain into another body, and at the end of the film we see him practising again under yet another false name. Frankenstein's climactic transformation into one of his own creations helps to clarify the film's attitude to him. The operation he has undergone is identical to that undergone by Karl; the outcome is more successful because of the nature of the patient.

Karl is weak and he is overwhelmed by the flesh, but Frankenstein's mind is strong and he will be able to control his new body (which, underlining his sense of his own perfection, is exactly the same as his original body). The dichotomy set up here between a domineering will and a flesh that is degrading and animalistic is one that informs a lot of Fisher's horrors, especially in their treatment of sexuality. *The Revenge of Frankenstein* is remarkably sex-free, but it is clear that Frankenstein's ambitions ultimately lead to the mastery and transcendence of the physical, and that this imperative too defines the way in which Karl is represented. For all the sympathy endowed upon him, Karl is just too much body and not enough mind.

To gain some sense of the subtlety of Fisher's approach to this material, it is useful briefly to compare the film with two other 'rogue scientist' films made in the late 1950s, *Blood of the Vampire* (1959: like *The Revenge of Frankenstein* this was written by Jimmy Sangster and, despite its title, is not a vampire movie) and *Corridors of Blood* (1959 but not released until the early 1960s). The first of these combines a bombastic condemnation of the cruel Frankenstein-like scientist with a lip-smacking relish over his monstrous activities. The second tells of a scientist attempting to develop anaesthetics who falls under the malign influence of some criminals; it is altogether more sober and measured than *Blood of the Vampire* and, perhaps because of this, is a worthy but rather dull affair. In comparison, *The Revenge of Frankenstein* is much more aware of the nuances and complexities in its subject. It neither condemns nor praises the Baron but instead seeks to make us aware of the human cost of his experiments even as it is drawn to his certainty and his indomitable will.

The two other films directed by Fisher during 1958 – *The Hound of the Baskervilles* and *The Man Who Could Cheat Death* (both released in 1959) – are of less consequence, although the Sherlock Holmes film does have its points of interest. For one thing, it was the first Hammer horror film to be set entirely in Britain (although *The Revenge of Frankenstein* concluded with a brief sequence in London). For another, it has a remarkable opening sequence. A depiction of 'the legend of the Hound of the

Baskervilles', it tells the story of Sir Hugo Baskerville, a decadent aristocrat who, after having murdered a local peasant girl, is himself killed by the eponymous hound. As is often the case in this most prolific part of his career, Fisher re-uses techniques that have worked for him before but relocates them within contexts where their meanings are modified. So yet again we have a lone figure advancing through the set towards the camera, in this case an enraged Sir Hugo who in one long uninterrupted take is shown moving from the head of the stairs down into the hall and eventually into extreme close-up as he screams, 'The hounds – let loose the pack!' It is a powerful moment which conveys in the most direct way Sir Hugo's maniacal energy.

The ending of the sequence – which depicts the Hound's attack on Sir Hugo – is also interesting as much for what we don't see as what we do. In fact we are not shown the Hound at all but only Sir Hugo's reaction to it. We hear a low growling and Sir Hugo looks screen left. As the unseen hound attacks, the camera itself moves suddenly forward, miming the Hound's assault without actually showing it. This withholding of the monster's appearance is untypical for Fisher who usually makes a point of depicting the monster in detail. A feature of those few horror monsters who are kept entirely or mainly offscreen – in what Pascal Bonitzer has termed 'blind space' – is that they tend to have more power and are harder to contain than those monsters who more fully exist in the field of the visible.[21] Fisher's keeping the Hound in blind space therefore renders its power illimitable, uncontainable.

The problem with this is that in a narrative which demands that the monster be shown at the end, the results can never live up to the awesome thing that lives in blind space. Indeed, as was noted by many critics in the late 1950s, when the Hound, or at least the version of it conjured up by the villains, is revealed in *The Hound of the Baskervilles*, it is especially unimpressive, turning out to be just a dog in a mask.[22] To a certain extent, this anti-climactic narrative trajectory was bequeathed to the film-makers by Arthur Conan Doyle's original novel which dealt with the dispersal of a superstitious legend by Sherlock Holmes' ratiocinative powers. The problem was exacerbated by Hammer's treatment of the story, however, for in its attempt to remake the narrative as a horror story, the gothic elements were exaggerated.

One consequence of this is that the remainder of the film operates at a lower intensity than the striking opening sequence. However, the movement traced by the narrative from this sequence's feudal past to the altogether more bourgeois society in which Sir Henry (Christopher Lee) lives is interesting because it is also apparent in a number of Fisher's other early horror films. Notable in this respect are the moves from the castle setting of *The Curse of Frankenstein* to the urban, non-feudal setting of *The Revenge of Frankenstein*, and from Dracula's Transylvanian castle to the Holmwoods' middle-class world in *Dracula*. In each case, the feudal setting is one in which the powerful male – be this Dracula or Frankenstein – is free to do what he wants. Once transplanted to a bourgeois setting, however, he is compelled to hide or disguise himself. In the case of *The Hound of the Baskervilles*, the vile but powerful Sir Hugo is transformed into the much weaker (to the extent of having a congenital heart condition) Sir Henry. Moreover – and Fisher plays this feature of the film very subtly – Sir Henry exists in a world where, unlike in Sir Hugo's world, men seem to have become interchangeable and their identity accordingly uncertain. Near the beginning of the film Sir Henry mistakes Sherlock Holmes for the manager of the hotel where he is staying. This inaugurates a series of misunderstandings relating to male identity, with Dr Watson mistaken for Sir Henry by John Stapleton, Holmes mistaken by the local Bishop for a telescope repair man, and the escaped convict Selden mistaken by both Holmes and the Hound for Sir Henry. It is significant, perhaps, that while caught up in these various identity crises, Holmes himself never dons any of his famous disguises.[23]

Fisher, and Hammer horror in general, has sometimes been accused of – or praised for – an anti-aristocratic bias. Hammer historian Denis Meikle has gone so far as to state that late 1950s Hammer horror reflected 'the new tide of socialism rising in the land'.[24] Meikle's views are usually insightful, but this is a curious claim, both historically and in terms of the films. Britain had had a Conservative government since 1951 and would continue to do so until 1964, so it hardly seems reasonable to think of there being a tide of socialism rising in the late 1950s (and some might even argue that the 1964 election of Harold Wilson's Labour government was not an unequivocal triumph for socialist values). In addition to this, the films themselves cannot really be seen as embodying a socialist view. Fisher's horror films – and indeed much of his earlier work – routinely represents members of the working class as animalistic (*The Revenge of Frankenstein*), as comic relief (*The Mummy*) or as passive victims (*The Hound of the Baskervilles*). The bourgeois do not fare much better (although it could be argued that the films, and the company that produced them, do embody certain bourgeois values).[25] The emphasis in all these films tends to be on the individual male who might or might not be an aristocrat (Dracula and Frankenstein are, Sherlock Holmes and Van Helsing are not) but who in any event stands alone and to a certain extent exists on the margins of society. These men are figures of fascination for the films, and, as we have seen, Fisher's mise-en-scene is concerned to explore them in both their positive and their negative aspects.

So far in this account of Fisher, I have largely avoided placing the work in a social context. This is not because I think that such an exercise will be unproductive. Clearly these films can be related to, and in a way are illustrative of, social trends and changes. One could certainly see them as part of a wider reformulation of gender roles taking place in British cinema in the late 1950s and early 1960s (which would include the British New Wave and the early James Bond films), with this in turn connected with much broader shifts in social understandings of gender occurring in the same period. The principal danger in such an approach is that it can lead to a certain reductionism, an avoidance of complexity within particular films in order to make them fit into an overall social pattern. It seems to me necessary, especially in a director study, to attend to a film's aesthetic dimension, not only in order to form a judgement of it as a film (as opposed to it as a social-historical document) but also to gain a sense of how it actually functions. Any reading of Fisher's horror films which sees them as 'anti-aristocrat' simply fails to take into account the ambivalences and ambiguities accruing from these figures and the fact that they are treated differently from one film to another. In order to grasp these complexities, one needs to attend to the minutiae of the films, their mise-en-scene, their staging – in short, to think of them as artefacts.

It follows that any shared qualities – and Fisher's horror films do have elements in common – should be measured against how the films are different from each other. Seen in this light, *The Revenge of Frankenstein* and *The Hound of the Baskervilles* present a comparable view on masculinity and authority, but *Revenge*'s treatment of its subject is more complex and effective than that offered by *The Hound*, and both of them are considerably better than Fisher's final project from 1958, *The Man Who Could Cheat Death*. This film tells the story of Dr Bonner, a scientist who has discovered the secret of immortality and commits murder in order to obtain body parts that will help him keep old age at bay. Peter Cushing turned down the part of Bonner and was replaced by the German actor Anton Diffring, and both the script and the production seem less accomplished than was the case with previous Hammer efforts, as if the Hammer film-makers had simply exhausted themselves after a prolific outburst of activity. Fisher himself seems to have given up on the project and offers only the most perfunctory treatment of the drama. As has already been noted, Fisher's career up until this time had been characterised by a certain unevenness, and *The Man Who Could Cheat Death* is clearly a low-point after *The Revenge of Frankenstein* and *The Hound of the Baskervilles*. However, its shift away from a focus on authoritative males to more vulnerable (and, in the case of Dr Bonner, self-pitying) men is one that recurs in subsequent Fisher films.

The British abroad

A striking feature of Fisher's horror films up until 1959 is that while all but one (*The Hound of the Baskervilles*) are set outside Britain, there is virtually no engagement in any of them with 'foreignness' as such. Virtually everyone speaks with an impeccable British (or, to be specific, English) accent, whether or not their characters are meant to be British. This changes in 1959 when Fisher directs *The Mummy* and *The Stranglers of Bombay*, two films which take explicitly as their subject encounters between Britishness and the foreign. British fiction, literary and cinematic, offers numerous examples of such encounters, especially in the context of representations of the British Empire. Broadly (and also crudely) speaking, these encounters tend to have two possible outcomes. The first is the reinforcement of a sense of British racial superiority in comparison with a foreign culture perceived as inferior, either childlike or savage or both. (The 1935 film version of *Sanders of the River* is a good example.) The other outcome involves a destabilisation of any sense of British superiority as the limitations of Britishness are revealed via its interchange with a non-British culture. (Raj fictions *The Jewel in the Crown* and *A Passage to India* spring to mind here.) Ultimately, perhaps, these two outcomes are not readily separable, and all of these fictional encounters can be seen to involve the management of anxieties about national and racial difference. It is also too facile simply to label those fictions which seek to establish British superiority as 'racist' while other more interrogative texts are 'progressive'. In fact, potentially racist attitudes permeate this whole area of cultural activity, especially in the way that British viewpoints and experiences tend to be privileged over the viewpoints and experiences of other nations and races. So far as Fisher's two films are concerned, *The Stranglers of Bombay* offers a half-hearted, qualified and somewhat confused defence of certain aspects of British rule in India while the more interesting *The Mummy* traces the collapse of British authority. Having said this, both share similar views on foreigners, be these Indian or Egyptian; these other cultures are consistently presented as involving a savage and ritualistic set of beliefs lurking beneath a deceptive veneer of civilised behaviour. Both too see British authority entirely in terms of masculinity. This latter feature is hardly unique to Fisher's films of course, but the focus here on the male and his authority (or lack thereof) helps to link these films with the preceding Hammer horrors and enables

Fisher to play further variations on themes he has already made his own.

Of the two films, *The Stranglers of Bombay* is the least impressive. In certain respects, it was not a typical film for either Fisher or Hammer. For one thing, it was shot in black and white; for another it was based – albeit very loosely – on a real historical event, the suppression of the Thugee cult in India by the East India Company in the early nineteenth century. In part, it can be seen as one of Hammer's periodic attempts to diversify away from its colour gothic output.[26] At the same time, it appears to have been marketed if not as a horror film per se then as a film very much like the previous gothic horrors: 'Filmed in Strangloscope' screamed its lurid poster. Fisher himself dismissed the film: '*Stranglers of Bombay* went wrong. It was too crude.'[27] The critics were also unkind: one, clearly not a Hammer fan, described it both as 'a particularly bestial contribution to the Hammer horror cycle' and as 'the usual fleabitten affair',[28] while another asked why anyone would want to be involved in the production of 'such perversion of the word "entertainment"'.[29]

Fisher was probably right to think of the film as crude; there is certainly something 'unfinished' about it, with potentially interesting themes and issues only half-addressed. This is most apparent in the film's treatment of British officialdom. Fisher gives us two Captains in the service of the East India Company – the efficient Captain Lewis who understands the Indian people and works tirelessly to uncover the Thugee plot, and the arrogant, incompetent Captain Connaught-Smith who shows no understanding whatsoever of India. This division is presented in class terms – with Connaught-Smith clearly having gained his position through belonging to the right sort of family and attending the right school; indeed he is apparently given command of Lewis's investigation because his father went to the same school as Lewis's commanding officer. (In comparison, Lewis has money worries and apparently has no significant family connections to fall back on.) Unsurprisingly, given the film's contemptuous treatment of him, Connaught-Smith ends badly, screaming in terror as his men are massacred around him.

However, Lewis himself (especially as played by the rather patrician and decidedly middle-class Guy Rolfe) turns out to be not entirely different from Connaught-Smith. He might be a bit nicer to the natives but only in a very condescending way. When his faithful servant Ram Das mysteriously disappears, Lewis shows about as much concern as one might for a missing family dog, and he actually seems fonder of Ram Das's pet mongoose than he does of Ram Das himself. The problem for the film is that it never manages to offer a coherent perspective on Lewis. In some scenes, he is the meritocratic figure (not a million miles away from Frankenstein or Van Helsing) who challenges the class-bound snobbery embodied by Connaught-Smith and poses awkward questions for the British establishment in general. For example, at one point he asks his commanding officer 'What real effort has the company made to stabilise India beyond what was just necessary to conduct its business?' (a question which, significantly, remains unanswered). But in other scenes he is 'better' than Connaught-Smith only because he is a more effective ruler (or oppressor) of the Indian population.

The film's representation of the Indians is similarly unresolved. On the one hand, there is the blind subservience of Ram Das, and on the other hand there is the irrational fanaticism of the Thugees. Having said this, there is one remarkable sequence which shows a Thugee leader coaching an acolyte on how to appear subservient and thereby win the trust of white men (a technique eventually used with fatal consequences on the witless Connaught-Smith). Here the subservience embodied by Ram Das is effectively 'de-naturalised', turned potentially into a performance hiding ⊦ feelings about the white oppressor. But in the end, as ⅰⁿ the case with this film, nothing is made of this, aⁿ ' to his death a dutiful servant.

It is interesting to compare *The Strai* other films dealing with the Thugees, *Iɲ of Doom* (1984) and *The Deceivers* (198 least the virtue of consistency in its ' pollutant of the white male Americ ultimately be overcome and white heⅰ think of another film so obsessed with poison, disgusting foreign food and purgative floods.) In contrast, the underrated *The Deceivers* portrays a British officer discovering a propensity for violence within himself as a result of his encounter with the Thugees, and there is a clear sense at the end of this film of British heroism undermined. In its various confusions, *The Stranglers of Bombay* manages to avoid both the simplicity of *Temple of Doom* and the complexity of *The Deceivers*. It concludes with a thoughtful Lewis stroking Ram Das's mongoose. The message should be clear – India has been tamed, domesticated. However, by this stage in the film there are simply too many unanswered questions and unresolved issues for this to feel even remotely like a coherent (albeit racist) ending.

One could reasonably relate these various uncertainties about Britishness to a broader cultural difficulty in representing the British Empire during the post-war period, when that empire was very visibly coming to an end. So far as understanding Fisher's career is concerned, however, it is probably more useful and relevant to think about the film's inadequacies in relation to Hammer's breakneck rate of production in the late 1950s and early 1960s. With limited pre-production and production schedules, there was simply insufficient time for the film-makers to reflect upon and mould their subject material into a coherent form. This seemed to matter less for the horror films as here Fisher and his colleagues could fall back on an established formulaic approach. When breaking new ground was required – as was the case with *The Stranglers of Bombay* – problems inevitably arose.

The Mummy, made immediately before *The Stranglers of Bombay*, also shows signs of being a rushed production, not least in its slapdash plot construction. As has been noted by horror historians, the film borrows both story elements and character names from several of Universal's *Mummy* films from the 1930s and 1940s, and it links these together in a manner that does not always make sense.[31] Characters are ignorant of something in one scene only to be aware of it later on, the Mummy is impervious to gunfire early on but succumbs to it in the conclusion, and, inexplicably, the 'locals' in the English-set scenes turn out to be Irish.

Despite these inconsistencies, *The Mummy* proves to be considerably more coherent, in thematic terms at least, than *The Stranglers of Bombay*, especially in its representation of masculinity. In *The Mummy*, all men are either physically injured (John Banning – played by Peter Cushing – with a lame leg, Kharis/The Mummy – played by Christopher Lee – with a ripped-out tongue), bumbling (Stephen Banning, John's father) or closed-minded (Joseph Whemple and, to a certain extent, the Egyptian high priest). In the context of this general weakness, the archaeologist Stephen Banning's dismissal of the priest's warning against entering Princess Ananka's tomb speaks not of an innate British superiority but rather is figured as arrogant and presumptuous (as is quickly demonstrated by Stephen's going mad at the mere sight of the resurrected Mummy). Far from establishing or reinforcing British authority, *The Mummy*'s opening depiction of an ill-fated British expedition abroad undermines it.[32] The scenes that follow then do something that *The Stranglers of Bombay* never does – they return us to England. This sudden transition is, in its own quiet way, as effective as the fade from Iraq to Washington DC that occurs in the American horror film *The Exorcist* (1973). In each case, we are given a clear and ominous sense that something alien is about to arrive in the homeland. This manoeuvre – this bringing the monster back home – can also be found in other gothic texts (one thinks in particular of the novel *Dracula*), although the immediacy of the transition from foreign climes to the English countryside apparent in *The Mummy* – with the long journey between the two locations elided – registers more powerfully the imminence of the threat than do the various literary versions.

While *The Stranglers of Bombay* offers a scenario in which the British seek to impose their values on another culture, *The Mummy* shows an England haunted and transformed by a sense of the foreign. Indeed what Fisher sets out to do most effectively in *The Mummy* is make the English landscape itself appear unhomely and threatening. This is partly achieved through the mere presence of 'foreign' elements – notably Kharis/The Mummy – within England. Scenes showing the Mummy striding through the countryside or crashing through John Banning's mansion-like house set up incongruous juxtapositions of the familiar – a cosy, domesticated Englishness – and the jarringly strange – an ancient Egyptian culture. These scenes also benefit immeasurably from Fisher's by now characteristic refusal of expressive exaggeration. Instead he deploys a matter-of-fact mise-en-scene full of longish takes and medium shots which emphasises both the solidity of the environment and the relentless physicality of the alien intrusion into it.

Yet there is more to *The Mummy* than a simple representation of a foreign invasion, for the film also suggests that these foreign elements relate to – and to a certain extent are themselves an expression of – things already gone wrong within the male psyche. That there is a flaw in the British male is apparent from the film's beginning, with Stephen Banning's sudden and total collapse into insanity a decidedly excessive response to the Mummy's resurrection. Appropriately, when we do arrive in England, the first thing we see is not, as one might have expected, John Banning's home but instead the lunatic asylum in which Stephen Banning lives (and John Banning himself turns out to be a less than effective hero who in the end has to rely on others to defeat the Mummy). This asylum subsequently provides the setting for a particularly effective dramatisation of what can only be described as an outburst of male hysteria, the likes of which had not been seen before in a Fisher film. Stephen Banning is alone in his cell when, as if he can somehow sense the presence of the Mummy nearby, he becomes frightened and starts to scream. This is intercut with the horse-drawn carriage delivering 'ancient relics' (i.e. Kharis/The Mummy) to the high priest as it passes by outside the asylum. Rarely for Fisher, tilted camera angles are used when filming Stephen Banning, stressing the extremity of his mental state.[33] The sound of his screaming causes the carriage-drivers to panic, they in turn lose control of the carriage, and the trunk containing Kharis is accidentally pitched into what locals later describe as a bottomless swamp (from which Kharis will later rise, summoned by the high priest). In its conjoining of the asylum, the swamp, and male panic, the sequence orchestrates a veritable symphony of male subjection and loss of control, and in this it can be seen to sum up the film as a whole, both thematically and in terms of its overall tone.

No cause is given for this male inadequacy. In *The Mummy*'s world, it appears that men are just like that, and this applies as much for Ancient Egypt as it does for Victorian England. Both of the film's flashbacks – the first showing Kharis having his tongue removed and then his being buried alive, the second depicting the onset of Stephen Banning's insanity – stress male disempowerment. It seems from this that the same story of disempowerment is being repeated – in Ancient Egypt, in the British invasion of Ananka's tomb, and then in England itself. Freud's description of the uncanny as that class of the frightening that 'in reality [is] nothing new or alien, but something which is familiar and old-established in the mind and which has become alienated from it only through the process of repression' seems particularly apt for *The Mummy* in its obsessive drawing of parallels between Egypt and England.[34] It follows that when John Banning confronts Kharis, he is in a sense coming face to face not so much with an enemy alien as with an image of himself and his own inadequacy, as is underlined by the fact that both Isabel, Banning's wife, and Ananka, Kharis's love, are played by the same woman (Yvonne Furneaux).[35]

Ultimately *The Mummy* tells us nothing about Egypt, but it does systematically undermine the male authority upon which any 'superior' British reading of Egyptian culture could be founded (something that *The Stranglers of Bombay* singularly fails to do), and in this it represents a significant achievement. Even as it does this, *The Mummy* preserves a sense of mystery about the reasons for this failure of the masculine. An image of the bottomless swamp provides an enigmatic conclusion to a film that in many respects is the antithesis of the more obviously pro-authority *Dracula* and *The Revenge of Frankenstein*. As we will see, in his next few films Fisher would explore further this theme of male powerlessness.

A tear in the eye

Hammer's relentless rate of production continued unabated through 1960: between 23 November 1959 when Fisher commenced shooting *The Two Faces of Dr Jekyll* (US: *House of Fright*) and 2 November 1960 when he finished shooting *The Curse of the Werewolf*, he managed to complete four feature films, *The Brides of Dracula* and *Sword of Sherwood Forest* plus the two titles given above. Fisher had by this stage gained considerable experience of making gothic horrors, and his continued involvement in this area afforded him numerous opportunities not only to re-use methods of staging and filming the dramas but also to develop and elaborate upon these. At the same time, and perhaps inevitably given the cramped and hurried circumstances of production, there was a noticeable inconsistency in the work with the director saving his energies for set pieces within and sections of particular films rather than focusing on any film as a whole.

Perhaps the best example from this period of both a reliance on set pieces and a refinement of previously used material is *The Brides of Dracula*, a sequel of sorts to *Dracula* (albeit one in which Dracula himself does not actually appear). The screenplay had had a complicated genesis. It was originally penned by Jimmy Sangster as a film that would feature Dracula. However, when it became apparent that Christopher Lee, keen to avoid type-casting, did not want to return to the role so shortly after the first film, the screenplay was rewritten as a non-Dracula vampire film by Peter Bryan (who had earlier written Fisher's *The Hound of the Baskervilles*), received a polish from Edward Percy and then was revised again by producer Anthony Hinds (although Hinds does not receive a credit, either under his own name or his writing pseudonym John Elder). The end result was, frankly, something of a mess, and, if anything, less coherent in story terms than *The Mummy*. Plot inconsistencies are so numerous as to be quite distracting. For example, why is the film's heroine Marianne surprised to hear of Baroness Meinster's death when earlier in the film she had seen the Baroness's corpse? (One suspects that this particular inconsistency might derive from the fact that in an earlier version of the screenplay Marianne had been two separate characters.) Or why does the school headmaster accept without question that Baron Meinster is who he says he is when it has earlier been made clear that everyone thinks the Baron is dead? And, most puzzling of all, if the vampiric Baron Meinster can transform himself into a bat (as apparently he can in this film), why does he need Marianne to unlock his chains when presumably he could just turn into a bat and fly away? As Fisher himself repeated in interviews, he rarely had much input into the screenplay but instead filmed what he was given, and clearly what he was given in *The Brides of Dracula* did not make much sense as a story. The director's response was to produce a film comprised of a series of remarkable and in some instances brilliantly executed set pieces.

Most impressive of all in this respect is the film's opening section, in which a young, innocent schoolteacher, Marianne Danielle, is lured to the Castle Meinster where she encounters the vampire Baron and his mother, the Baroness. For the first time in his Hammer horror work, Fisher has a female as his central protagonist, and in depicting her attempts to uncover the mystery of the Castle Meinster, the film is more than a little reminiscent of that other Fisher 'female gothic' *So Long at the Fair* (although, unsurprisingly, Van Helsing's eventual arrival results in Marianne's marginalisation and her subordination to his authority). This part of the film serves a similar function to the opening of *Dracula* where Jonathan Harker first encounters the vampire. Both Harker's weakness and Marianne's ignorance of vampires serve to under-line Van Helsing's strength and knowledge when he does show up. In *The Brides of Dracula*, however, the directorial attention to detail and atmosphere far exceeds this function. The scenes depicting the peasants in the inn are longer and more subtle than the equivalent scenes in *Dracula*, especially in their presentation of the peasants' vacillation between fear of the vampire and compassion for Marianne. Similarly the castle itself is a far more grandiose location than Dracula's castle, larger, more elaborately designed and altogether more mysterious. Fisher's staging of the action is also impressive. This book has already made something of Fisher's ability to create a meaningful dramatic relationship between the movements of the film's characters and the movements of the camera, and this ability is more than apparent in *The Bride of Dracula*'s opening scenes. One thinks here of the Baroness's movement through the inn at which Marianne has been stranded. As she is leaving with Marianne, her turning back to the younger woman, when coupled with the sudden acceleration forwards of the camera tracking her progress, gives us a sense of her imperious authority far more effectively than any dialogue could. Later, the transference of power from the Baroness to her evil son is represented by a comparable co-ordination of camera and character movement. When Marianne runs down the castle stairs away from the Baroness, the camera is positioned at the bottom of the stairs. As Marianne, moving right to left at a diagonal angle to the camera, passes by, the camera pans to follow her. This pan suddenly reveals the Baron as Marianne runs into his arms. The Baron's unexpected appearance here – Marianne appeared not to be running to anyone but rather attempting to escape from the Baroness – bestows upon him a Dracula-like power over off-screen space that up until this point, chained by his mother, he had lacked. Moreover, the combination of Marianne's fearful flight, the Baroness's terror and the Baron's calmness and immobility produce an unnerving sense of both great power and extreme subjection. Similarly themed set pieces include the Baroness's demented maid encouraging a neophyte vampire to claw her way out of her grave in a grim parody of the birthing process, and Van Helsing, having received a vampire bite, 'cleansing' the wound with a red-hot iron. In each case, we find a representation of the flesh as something that either dominates the individual – via the instinctive drive of the vampire – or which, with sufficient will-power (i.e., Van Helsing's will-power), can be mastered.

An interesting feature of *The Brides of Dracula* that perhaps does not sit so easily with Fisher's way of doing things lies in the characterisation of Baron Meinster himself who is younger looking than Dracula (although David Peel, the actor who played him, was forty at the time of production) and still lives with his mother. While one would not want to make too much of this (the film certainly doesn't), the fact that his vampirism is presented as an affliction arising from his being indulged by his mother, plus a certain campness in David Peel's performance, do suggest a potentially gay – albeit stereotypically gay – dimension to the proceedings. It is significant in this respect that while the 1958 *Dracula* was extremely circumspect about Dracula vampirising Harker (i.e. it didn't show the act at all), *The Brides of Dracula* does have a scene in which Meinster bites Van Helsing. The act of biting is concealed from us by Meinster's cloak, but given that the vampire's bite or 'kiss' is generally presented as an erotic act, the raised cloak might conceivably be seen as a censoring device, covering something un-representable.[36] A number of critics have identified a homoerotic dimension in the novel *Dracula* (and in some of its cinematic adaptations); for example, Christopher Craft has argued that 'the sexual threat that this novel first evokes, manipulates, sustains, but never finally represents is that Dracula will seduce, penetrate, drain another male'.[37] Of all Hammer's Dracula films, *The Brides of Dracula* is the one that most clearly poses the possibility of homoerotic desire.[38] However, as was the case with the homoerotic aspects of *The Astonished Heart*, Fisher seems distant from, uninterested in, or perhaps even unaware of these elements (although the cloak covering Meinster's biting/ kissing Van Helsing suggests a certain discomfort on the part of the film-makers).[39] Refusing the play with gender that one finds elsewhere in horror – not just in the work of gay directors such as James Whale but also, say, in Roger Corman's Poe films or the Italian work of Dario Argento – Fisher, as he had done before, addresses the heterosexual features of the scenario, maps these on to an authority-subjection relationship, and ignores everything else.

Of the three other films completed by Fisher during 1960, the most negligible is *Sword of Sherwood Forest*. The second of three Robin Hood features produced by Hammer (the others were *Men of Sherwood Forest* in 1954 and *A Challenge for Robin Hood* in 1967) and the only one directed by Fisher, it featured Richard Greene, who had starred as Robin in the successful 1950s TV series *The Adventures of Robin Hood*, a series upon which Fisher himself had worked.[40] The film turned out to be a listless, meandering affair, and Fisher's direction competent but little more. If nothing else, *Sword of Sherwood Forest* underlined the extent to which Fisher's abilities as a director had become focused on horror and fantasy projects.

In the case of another of Fisher's 1960 films, *The Two Faces of Dr Jekyll*, one finds a very self-conscious and ambitious attempt to update the well-known story by making the monstrous Hyde more physically attractive than the sullen, hirsute Dr Jekyll. David Pirie has seen this as reflecting Fisher's view of things: 'In Fisher's work evil is usually highly attractive on the surface ... At times, as in the Frankenstein series or in *Dr Jekyll*, the two opposing forces clash in one man and the result is highly ambiguous but usually ultimately destructive.'[41] However, the film's uneasy, faltering treatment of this idea suggests that Fisher was unsure what to do with it. There is a similar lack of clarity in the film's treatment of women. *The Two Faces of Dr Jekyll* continues the tradition initiated by stage adaptations of Robert Louis Stevenson's original novel and maintained in the 1932 and 1941 American film versions of surrounding Jekyll with women; the novel, by contrast, dealt exclusively with male/male relationships. In previous film versions this involved the contrasting pairing of a 'good' woman (i.e. virginal, middle-class, usually Jekyll's fiancée) and a 'fallen' women (i.e. sexually active, working-class, usually a prostitute ill-used and ultimately murdered by Hyde). Hammer's version modifies this: it still has the prostitute (although more 'up-market' here than in earlier films) but the 'good' woman turns out to be Jekyll's wife, already sexually experienced and in the midst of an affair with Jekyll's best friend. The film also suggests an interchangeability between the two women – the prostitute is murdered by Jekyll/Hyde as she lies in Mrs Jekyll's bed while Mrs Jekyll commits suicide in the brothel after having been raped by her husband. This transposition is so blatant that it is obviously meant to signify something, but what that something might be is not immediately apparent. If isolated from the rest of the film, one might read it as a criticism of Victorian hypocrisy and double standards. However, unlike its cinematic predecessors, Fisher's film barely engages at all with the idea of Victorian England as a hypocritical society. Instead it tells the more domesticated story of a cuckolded husband seeking revenge on his wife and her lover.

The film's key ideas – Hyde being more attractive than Jekyll, the transposition of the women – emerge from this as essentially intellectual conceits only partly connected with the main narrative. One senses on Fisher's part a discomfort with these 'intellectual' elements. 'Personally I would have written it differently', he said of the screenplay in a 1964 interview, 'made him [Jekyll/Hyde] more horrible *and* given him some redeeming features. But that was the written word.'[42] Later, in an interview he gave in 1975, he complained that 'You didn't have a single character in that story who was worth tuppence ha'penny', but also stated 'I liked the script. I think Wolf Mankowitz wrote it partly from the point of view that Victorian England was corrupt. But it wasn't fundamentally a very deep script, was it?'[43] Presented with a screenplay which, despite being more coherent as a narrative than *The Brides of Dracula*, did not afford Fisher the 'emotional' possibilities of previous screenplays (and in a production schedule that gave him virtually no time to develop the screenplay), the director seemed at something of a loss. As he had done before when confronted with similarly unamenable material, he offered a competent but undistinguished treatment of the drama.

John Elder's screenplay for *The Curse of Werewolf*, an adaptation of Guy Endore's 1933 novel *The Werewolf of Paris*, appears to have been more to Fisher's taste. A sprawling narrative running through three generations, it is less tightly structured than *The Two Faces of Dr Jekyll* but considerably more cohesive than *The Brides of Dracula*. In particular, Fisher highlights the way that *The Curse of the Werewolf* (which was to be his fourth and final 1960 project) is structured around a series of repetitions. The story of Leon, the werewolf (played by a young Oliver Reed who also had small roles in *The Two Faces of Dr Jekyll* and *Sword of Sherwood Forest*) is told in two segments, the first when he is a child, the second an adult. In each segment he is shot with the same silver bullet, wounded in the first instance, killed in the second. Each of these segments takes place mainly in the same small Spanish town with the same actors (including Hammer regulars Michael Ripper and George

Woodbridge) appearing twice-over. As already noted in respect of *The Mummy*, repetition of this kind has potentially an uncanny dimension; here the return to the same location and the same faces also gives Fisher an opportunity to illustrate the process of ageing and decay, with the inhabitants of the town considerably the worse for wear on our second visit to them.

A similar stress on the passing of years and an accompanying physical degradation is also apparent in *The Curse of the Werewolf*'s opening scenes which detail the genesis of the werewolf. To a certain extent, this part of the film replays the opening of *The Hound of the Baskervilles*, with a decadent aristocrat (Sir Hugo in *The Hound*, the Marques in *The Curse of the Werewolf*) torturing and generally ill-using peasants. However, *The Curse of the Werewolf* presents a more elaborate version. The evil Marques consigns a beggar to the dungeon because the beggar, with a leering expression on his face, has disrespectfully wished the Marques a good time on his wedding night. Years later, the beggar has become a feral creature while the Marques appears to be in the advanced stages of syphilis. When the gaoler's beautiful mute daughter rejects the Marques's sexual advances, he has her thrown into the dungeon where she is raped by the beggar (who then dies). She then stabs the Marques to death and, pregnant with the werewolf Leon, escapes into the forest.[44] From their first appearances, both the Marques and the beggar are defined in terms of their physical appetites, whether this be for food, sex, or a combination of the two; and the passing of time transforms them both into disgusting figures whose decaying bodies signify their surrender to the physical. Fisher takes a perverse pleasure in detailing their decay, for instance in the scene where the aged Marques picks a piece of rotting skin away from his face.

The remainder of the film deals with Leon's struggle to transcend the flesh and deal with a body that periodically, when the moon is full, revolts against his will, with this revolt very much associated with sexuality (with a key transformation taking place in a brothel). In previous Fisher films, the counter to the threat of the physical was the indomitable will of a male authority figure (e.g. Van Helsing or Frankenstein). Here there is no such authority figure, and instead the film poses the love of a good woman as the solution to Leon's problem. However, despite Fisher's claim that *The Curse of the Werewolf* was 'fundamentally a very tragic love story',[45] the relationship between Leon and Cristina, his employer's daughter, is not presented with much conviction or energy, and in this it anticipates similarly vapid romantic couples in Fisher's later work (notably *The Phantom of the Opera*, *The Earth Dies Screaming* and *Dracula – Prince of Darkness*). Given this, it is perhaps not surprising that this love fails to save Leon from his animal nature and eventually he is destroyed by his adoptive father. A close-up of Leon's dead body shows that there were tears in his eyes when he died, a sentimental detail anticipated by the film's opening credits which featured an extreme close-up of Leon's eyes as tears run from them.

These images of a man crying are sufficiently unusual both for horror cinema and British cinema in this period to merit some comment. Tears of this kind speak of a lack of male control and a 'feminine' surrender to subjection. It has already been noted that many of Fisher's horror films – and indeed some of his pre-horror work as well – depend on what I have termed an authority-subjection nexus. Authority here is associated with the exercise of the will and an ability to transcend the flesh (hence the celibacy of many Fisher heroes) while subjection is connected above all else with the body, the flesh, sexuality. There is a mutually defining relationship between authority and subjection apparent within certain Fisher films – one thinks here in particular of the powerful Frankenstein and the powerless Karl in *The Revenge of Frankenstein* – but authority and subjection are also concepts that separate out the films from each other, with *The Man Who Could Cheat Death*, *The Mummy* and *The Curse of the Werewolf* more open to an exploration of subjection than the authoritative Dracula and Frankenstein films. Throughout his horror work, Fisher seems more engaged with those scenarios that permit him to dramatise authority and subjection, both in interaction and separately, and his mise-en-scene develops to provide vivid pictures of each.

Fisher's next film was *The Phantom of the Opera*. Made a full year after *The Curse of the Werewolf* (with the shoot running from

November 1961 to January 1962), it is in many respects a rather timid reworking of that earlier film. Again we have a figure, here the Phantom, characterised by a lack of control who dies with tears in his eyes, and a dull romantic couple about whom we care little. The timidity arguably derives from Hammer's intention to make a film with a broader appeal than its previous gothics (which meant both a bigger budget than usual and a softening of the horror elements). The resulting film generated an effective atmosphere, but Fisher could not do much with a laborious plot. Moreover, it did not do well at the box office, and its failure seems to have produced a certain cooling of relations between Fisher and Hammer (although he continued to work for the company). Hammer's next two gothic horrors – *Kiss of the Vampire* (1964) and *The Evil of Frankenstein* (1964) – would not be directed by Fisher, and Fisher himself, for the first time since 1957, would start to make films away from Hammer. This part of his career had come to an end.

The 1957–1962 period was crucial for Fisher. It saw the production of some of his best-known films and established the basis for his subsequent reputation. This chapter has argued that it was a period of considerable achievement for the director. Of course, the work he produced was not of a consistent standard, but given both the limited resources available to him and the rapidity of production, it is remarkable that he managed to achieve anything at all. In essence, what the Hammer gothic film-makers – Fisher key amongst them – did in these few years was create a separate, self-defining world, a world of desire and subjection, of authority and power. Fisher's mise-en-scene helped to make that world come alive; it endowed it both with a solidity and with a stylised fairy tale-like quality. If Fisher had not made another film after *The Phantom of the Opera*, one feels that there would still have been sufficient evidence to make a case for him as a film-maker of distinction and worth (although whether everyone would have accepted this case is another matter). But Fisher had not finished, and some remarkable work was yet to come.

Notes

1 Harry Ringel, 'Terence Fisher underlining', *Cinefantastique*, 4:3 (1975), p. 22.
2 For dates of principal photography of Fisher's Hammer horror films, see Marcus Hearn and Alan Barnes, *The Hammer Story* (London, Titan), 1997.
3 For information on Hammer, see in particular Dennis Meikle's splendid history of the studio, *A History of Horrors: The Rise and Fall of the House of Hammer* (Lanham, MD, and London, Scarecrow Press), 1996.
4 *The Observer*, 5 May 1957.
5 *The Daily Telegraph*, 4 May 1957.
6 For a fuller discussion of the press response to Hammer, see Peter Hutchings, *Hammer and Beyond: The British Horror Film* (Manchester, Manchester University Press), 1993, pp. 4–11.
7 David Pirie, *A Heritage of Horror: The English Gothic Cinema 1946–1972* (London, Gordon Fraser), 1973, p. 50.
8 The 1930s versions of *Dracula* and *Frankenstein* had been re-released in Britain in the mid-1950s and consequently would have been familiar to many in the British audience for Hammer's film.
9 Interestingly, this scene is 'quoted' in Stanley Kubrick's film version of *Lolita* (1962). Near the beginning of the film, there is an abrupt cut from Humbert's first view of Lolita to the Creature's first appearance in *The Curse of Frankenstein*. Only after a few seconds do we realise that Humbert, Lolita and her mother are in a drive-in cinema watching the Hammer film. Here Kubrick seems to have recognised the 'shock value' of Fisher's work and uses it to say something about Humbert's relation to Lolita. (I leave it to the reader to decide what.)

   So far as shock effects in horror generally are concerned, they were, of course, present in the genre before Fisher came along; one thinks in particular here of the famous 'bus' moment from Val Lewton's 1942 production of *Cat People*. But the abruptness of the shock in *The Curse of Frankenstein* renders it markedly different, more arbitrary, less reliant on a suspenseful build-up.
10 Both photography and set design undoubtedly benefited from *Dracula*'s larger budget, up from *The Curse of Frankenstein*'s £65,000 to £81,000.
11 Gregory A. Waller, *The Living and the Undead: From Stoker's Dracula to Romero's Dawn of the Dead* (Urbana and Chicago, University of Illinois Press), 1986, p. 113.
12 Harker's arrival at the castle was preceded in Sangster's screenplay by a scene in a carriage where Harker is given various ominous warnings by his fellow passengers. It is not clear whether this sequence was filmed – we do catch a brief glimpse of a carriage just before Harker arrives at the castle – but in any event it was probably right for it to be dropped. It seems to be both a very conventional scene and an unnecessary slowing down of the action. The opening of the film as it stands is much more urgent and forceful.
13 Fisher himself must have been pleased with the shot; he repeats it – although to less effect – in his next film for Hammer, *The Revenge of Frankenstein*, for the scene in which the Baron first enters his laboratory,

and in a more tentative form in *The Gorgon* (1964) when Professor Heitz enters the Castle Borski.

14 It is difficult to find any film version of *Dracula* which is even remotely faithful to Stoker's sprawling original. Some film adaptations rely heavily on earlier stage adaptations while others lift selected elements from the novel and combine them with elements 'borrowed' from earlier Dracula films. Such is the creative process in the horror genre. For the record, the most faithful adaptation of the novel is probably the impressive 1977 BBC TV version featuring Louis Jourdan as the Count and Frank Finlay as Van Helsing.

15 For an interesting discussion of this in relation to the novel, see Richard Astle, 'Dracula as totemic monster: Lacan, Freud, Oedipus and history', *Substance*, 25 (1980), pp. 98–105.

16 Moments of male disempowerment that involve similar camera set-ups occur in Fisher's *The Hound of the Baskervilles* and *The Mummy*. For a discussion of the 'oedipal' qualities apparent in this, see Hutchings, *Hammer and Beyond*, pp. 70–82.

17 Terence Fisher: 'Dracula preyed upon the sexual frustrations of his woman victims. The (Holmwood) marriage was one in which she was not sexually satisfied and that was her weakness as far as Dracula's approach to her was concerned. When she arrived back after having been away all night she said it all in one close-up at the door ... I remember Melissa (Melissa Stribling who played Mina) saying "Terry how should I play the scene?" So I told her, "Listen, you should imagine you have had one whale of a sexual night, *the* one of your own sexual experience. Give me that in your face!"' Cited in *Dracula: The House that Hammer Built – Special Edition* (May 1998), p. 13.

18 Peter Cushing was a very active contributor to the films in which he appeared, frequently revising (or rewriting completely) his dialogue as well as suggesting various bits of business, as he did here with *Dracula*. For details of his contributions to Hammer films, see David Miller, *The Peter Cushing Companion* (London, Reynolds & Hearn), 2000.

19 *Films and Filming*, 4:6 (March 1958), p. 29.

20 Terence Fisher, 'Horror is my business', *Films and Filming*, 10:10 (July 1964), p. 8.

21 See Pascal Bonitzer, 'Partial vision: film and the labyrinth', *Wide Angle*, 4:4 (1981), pp. 56–64. In fact, many horror films depict the attempts of the forces of normality to bring the monster out from blind space into on-screen space in order to make it easier to destroy. One thinks here in particular of the American slasher film of the late 1970s and early 1980s (and Hammer's own psychological thrillers – such as *Taste of Fear* and *Paranoiac*).

22 In a desperate attempt to make this hound appear bigger, the Hammer film-makers had shot footage of it with some children made up to look like adults. Unsurprisingly, the end results were unconvincing and the experiment was discontinued.

23 It is also significant that *The Hound of the Baskervilles* boasts a female villain, Cecile, John Stapleton's daughter. It is never clear what part she

actually plays in the criminal conspiracy, but the presence of a powerful women in the film is clearly bound up with, and is a condition of, the presence of weak men elsewhere.

24 Meikle, *A History of Horrors*, p. 80.

25 For more on this, see Hutchings, *Hammer and Beyond*, pp. 66–8.

26 This impulse led Hammer into the production of thrillers, comedies and historical dramas.

27 Fisher, 'Horror is my business', p. 8.

28 *Monthly Film Bulletin*, 27:312 (January 1960), p. 10.

29 *Films and Filming*, 6:5 (February 1960), p. 23.

30 Before commencing production on *The Stranglers of Bombay*, Hammer had explored the possibility of making a film of John Masters' novel *The Deceivers*. However, screen rights had proved too expensive. *The Deceivers* was eventually brought to the screen as an Ismail Merchant production.

31 See Meikle, *A History of Horrors*, pp. 96–7 on sources for *The Mummy*; also interesting in this respect is the entry on 'Mummies' in Kim Newman (ed.), *The BFI Companion to Horror* (London, BFI), 1996, pp. 223–6.

32 Fisher's film does this far more systematically than the original 1932 Universal version of *The Mummy* in which the man who goes mad is young and impressionable and is clearly not meant to be seen as an authority figure.

33 Fisher's other extended use of tilted camera angles occurs in the flashback scene in *The Phantom of the Opera* where their main function is to separate out the events in the flashback from the rest of the film.

34 Sigmund Freud, 'The uncanny', in *The Penguin Freud Library: Volume 14 – Art and Literature* (Harmondsworth, Penguin), 1990, pp. 363–4.

35 There is a similar doubling of the female in the 1932 version of *The Mummy*, although there the resemblance is explained in terms of reincarnation. In Fisher's *The Mummy*, the resemblance is just a coincidence. One consequence of this is that Isabel becomes a much less significant figure who has very little to do in the film other than be looked at, threatened and finally saved. *The Mummy* might undermine male confidence but for all that it remains wholeheartedly male-centred. Not until later would Hammer – with *Blood from the Mummy's Tomb* (1971, based upon Bram Stoker's novel *Jewel of the Seven Stars*) – explore the theme of the reincarnated female.

36 When Baroness Meinster first appears as a vampire, she covers her fangs with a veil. Again the veil can be seen as a 'censoring' device, covering something that for the film is scandalous – in this case, the signs of desire and sexual hunger in the body of an old woman.

37 Christopher Craft, '"Kiss me with those red lips": gender and inversion in Bram Stoker's Dracula', in Glennis Byron (ed.), *Dracula* (London, Macmillan), 1999, p. 96.

38 After *Dracula* and *The Brides of Dracula*, these were *Dracula – Prince of Darkness* (1966, Fisher), *Dracula Has Risen From the Grave* (1968, Freddie Francis), *Taste the Blood of Dracula* (1970, Peter Sasdy), *The Scars of Dracula* (1970, Roy Ward Baker), *Dracula A. D. 1972* (1972, Alan Gibson) and *The Satanic Rites of Dracula* (1973, Gibson). In all cases Dracula was played by

Christopher Lee. The Count also appears briefly in *The Legend of the Seven Golden Vampires* (1974, Baker) where he was played by John Forbes-Robertson.

39 Bearing this in mind, it is interesting that there has been some gossip and speculation in fan publications about David Peel's sexuality. The extent to which this has been encouraged by the film itself is unclear, however.

40 This book has not engaged with the work that Fisher did for television in the 1950s – details of which are included in the Filmography. This is primarily because, so far as I am aware, very little of this material is available for viewing. The history of the part played by television in the careers of British film directors in the post-war period is yet to be written.

41 Pirie, *A Heritage of Horror*, p. 51.

42 Fisher, 'Horror is my business', p. 8.

43 Ringel, 'Terence Fisher underlining', p. 26.

44 Incidentally, this is yet another example of a movement away from an essentially feudal society to the more bourgeois world in which Leon will be brought up.

45 Ringel, 'Terence Fisher underlining', p. 22.

Highs and lows: 1962–72

4

Back in the early 1950s Terence Fisher had found himself exiled to the non-prestigious support-feature sector of the British film industry, and after the 1962 box-office failure of *The Phantom of the Opera* his career seemed to stall for a second time. He did not work for Hammer again for nearly two years, and of the eleven post-*Phantom* films he would go on to direct before his effective retirement in 1972 (although his final film would not be released until 1974) five would be for companies other than Hammer. After the phenomenal success of his Hammer horror films, some of the non-Hammer projects from the 1960s appear decidedly retrograde, harking back as they do to the sorts of films Fisher was making before he turned to horror. Two – *The Horror of it All* (1964) and *The Earth Dies Screaming* (1964) – were made for American producer Robert Lippert, who in the first part of the 1950s had had a production deal with Hammer; like those early Lippert-Hammer films – most of them thrillers and quite a few directed by Fisher – *The Horror of it All* and *The Earth Dies Screaming* featured imported American stars (Pat Boone and Willard Parker respectively). Another of Fisher's films from the early 1960s, *Sherlock Holmes and the Deadly Necklace* (1962), which was filmed in Germany, repeated the indignity of the co-directorial credits for *The Astonished Heart* and *So Long at the Fair* by crediting Fisher as co-director with Frank Winterstein (although, as with the earlier Antony Darnborough collaborations, the extent of Winterstein's involvement with the Sherlock Holmes film remains unclear). In addition to this, when Fisher did return to Hammer, he returned to a company that was in the process of changing. One of Fisher's key horror collaborators, the writer Jimmy Sangster, had moved on from writing gothic horrors in the early 1960s and was specialising in psychological thrillers, while the producer-writer Anthony Hinds, another very important figure in the formation of Hammer horror, had retired from active production duties in 1964 (although he continued as a writer); and in 1966 Hammer itself would move from Bray Studios, its base for sixteen years.

Bearing all this in mind, it is perhaps not surprising that the latter part of Fisher's film-making career has a certain fragmented quality to it, and that a review of his later films finds very significant achievements intermingling with some uninteresting work. We have seen this sort of unevenness before in Fisher's career as he moved from one area of British cinema to another – from Highbury to Gainsborough, from Gainsborough to pre-horror Hammer, and from there to Hammer horror – usually with little control over where he ended up. The difference here was that by the early 1960s Fisher had for the first time acquired a certain reputation in the industry. He was the Hammer horror man, and the projects he was offered at this stage, both by Hammer and other companies, reflected this perception of him inasmuch as they were all horror-related in some form or other. This was most obviously the case for the six remaining films at Hammer, all of which were gothics – *The Gorgon* (1964), *Dracula – Prince of Darkness* (1966), *Frankenstein Created Woman* (1967), *The Devil Rides Out* (1968), *Frankenstein Must Be Destroyed* (1969) and *Frankenstein and the Monster from Hell* (1974); and, as we will see, Fisher's three science fiction films from this period arguably operated more as horror than they did as science fiction.

As if to underline the break that occurs in Fisher's career between the stability of the 1957–1962 years at Hammer and the somewhat more unsettled post-1962 period, Fisher's two least accomplished late films come in the immediate aftermath of *The Phantom of the Opera* – the co-directed German production *Sherlock Holmes and the Deadly Necklace* and the Lippert-produced horror-comedy *The Horror of it All*. An evaluation of the Sherlock Holmes film is probably not helped by the execrable dubbing of the English-language version: robbing Christopher Lee (as Sherlock Holmes) and Thorley Walters (as Dr Watson) of their distinctive voices seems a much worse crime than what the villainous Moriarty is planning in the film itself. Even with an improved standard of dubbing, however, *Sherlock Holmes and the Deadly Necklace* would not be that interesting, thematically or stylistically. Its listless narrative – involving the usual Holmesian mix of mysterious murders and family secrets – contains no surprises, and the film as a whole, with its flat visual style, feels more like an extended episode of a rather mediocre television series than it does a piece of cinema. For all the brilliance of its opening sequence, Fisher's version of *The Hound of the Baskervilles* was one of the lesser Hammer horrors, but when placed alongside *Sherlock Holmes and the Deadly Necklace* it begins to look like a little masterpiece.

Sadly, *The Horror of it All* is not much better. Its narrative – in which an American outsider (played by popular singer Pat Boone) finds himself in a house populated by an eccentric family – owes more than a little, both in plot and tone, to James Whale's classic 1933 US horror *The Old Dark House* (which, despite its US origins, boasted a British setting and a predominantly British cast) and the British-produced *The Ghoul* (1933). *The Old Dark House* was remade (badly) by Hammer in 1962, and *The Ghoul* too was remade – this time very effectively – by director Pat Jackson as *What a Carve Up!* in 1961. Other British horror-comedies of the 'old dark house' type include the Frankie Howard vehicle *The House in Nightmare Park* (1973) and director Pete Walker's *The House of the Long Shadows* (1983). All of these rely – with varying degrees of effectiveness – on a fairly broad sense of macabre humour that seems quite alien to Fisher's work. This does not mean that Fisher's films are lacking in humour but instead that the humour there tends to be restricted to certain scenes or performances – one thinks of actor Miles Malleson's delightful cameo appearances in *Dracula*, *The Hound of the Baskervilles*, *The Brides of Dracula* and *The Phantom of the Opera* – and elsewhere held in check and kept in the background (the joke about the painting in *The Curse of Frankenstein*, for example). Perhaps because of this, *The Horror of it All* turns out to be the least of the 'old dark house' films; it's not funny and it's not frightening, and its presence along with *Sherlock Holmes and the Deadly Necklace* in the Fisher oeuvre did not bode well for the director's later films. However, in this final part of what had been an eventful career, Fisher was about to re-establish himself as a film-maker of some distinction.

Invasion

Between 1964 and 1967 Fisher directed three science fiction films, *The Earth Dies Screaming* (1964), *Island of Terror* (1966) and *The Night of the Big Heat* (1967). When these films are considered at all in discussions of Fisher's work, they are usually seen as minor and rather undistinguished addenda to the horror work that Fisher had done and was continuing to do at Hammer. As Fisher apologist Harry Ringel puts it: 'One is hard put to find ... Fisher in *The Earth Dies Screaming, Island of Terror* and *Island of the Burning Damned* (*Night of the Big Heat*). Stylistically, they replace Bernard Robinson's planned ornateness with indifferent location shooting. Thematically, they fall victim to the subordination-of-character-to-concept trap which science fiction so often sets, and which Fisher had worked so hard to avoid in his horror movies ... Not even Peter Cushing could enliven the flattened souls who inhabit Fisher's faintly imprinted science fiction universe.'[1] None of these films were made for Hammer – as noted above, *The Earth Dies Screaming* was for Robert Lippert while *Island of Terror* and *Night of the Big Heat* were produced by Tom Blakeley for Planet Films – and they lacked the production values associated with the modestly budgeted but still relatively more expensive Hammer horrors. As was the case with Fisher's pre-horror work (discussed in Chapter 2), there seems to be a problem here in relating these SF films to the horror films. They are just too different from the horrors – generically, stylistically, thematically – and largely because of this the SF films themselves are seen to lack significance and value. (As if to underline this, Fisher himself often expressed his dislike of the science fiction genre.)

I've already argued in Chapter 1 that seeing Fisher solely as a horror director can blind us to the way in which he constantly remade himself as a film-maker throughout his career, adjusting to the changing circumstances in which he had to work. Films like *To the Public Danger*, *Portrait from Life*, *Four Sided Triangle* and *Stolen Face* are interesting not only because they anticipate Fisher's later horror films but also because they offer something different from that work, something which is intrinsically worthwhile and which highlights different facets of Fisher's film-making skills. Much the same can be said for the three SF films from the 1960s. Certainly one can identify some elements in these films which link them to the rest of Fisher's work – not just the horror films but the pre-horror material as well – but they also represent something different for Fisher, a possible new direction for him. Of course, it won't do to over-value these films, but the fact that they are not gothic horrors and in some respects do not fit well with Fisher's horror work should not impede an appreciation of what interesting and distinctive features they do possess.

All three films tell stories of invasion – in *The Earth Dies Screaming* and *Night of the Big Heat* the invaders are extraterrestrial while in *Island of Terror* they are the unexpected by-product of a scientific experiment gone terribly wrong – and all three share certain properties with other British invasion fantasies of the 1960s. During the 1950s, Nigel Kneale's *Quatermass* TV series (all three of which were subsequently filmed by Hammer) and John Wyndham's SF invasion novels (*The Day of the Triffids*, *The Kraken Wakes* and *The Midwich Cuckoos*) had presented scenarios in which an extraterrestrial incursion escalated to a point where it threatened the whole nation and in some cases the whole world. The invasion fantasy as imagined by British film-makers in the 1960s and 1970s changes this in certain respects; in most of the films the threat of global escalation has receded and instead one finds invasion represented on a smaller, more intimate scale, often in terms of the domestic and the familial, and played out in isolated settings. So, for example, in *Invasion* (1966), the 'invasion' involves only three aliens who aren't particularly interested in Earth anyway and confine most of their activities to the grounds of a small country hospital; in *The Unearthly Stranger* (1963) the invading alien turns out to be the wife of the film's hero; and in *Prey* (1977) the film's sole alien restricts his activities to a lonely country house.[2] Fisher's SF invasion films obviously fit into this pattern – *The Earth Dies Screaming* is set in and around a small village, and *Island of Terror* and *Night of the Big Heat* both take place on islands cut off from the mainland. While it is suggested in *The Earth Dies Screaming* that the invasion might be global, the film restricts itself to events in the village; and in the two island films the islands themselves are bridgeheads for the invasion, with these invasions finally defeated on the islands without any significant help from the outside world. As with other 1960s SF films, isolation provides both the setting and the theme.

When one gets to the details of the films themselves, however, they start to take on a character of their own. Avoiding the spectacular paranoia of *The Unearthly Stranger* – which ultimately suggests that all women might be aliens – and the subdued realism of *Invasion* and *Prey*, Fisher's films opt for a more obviously studio-based approach interspersed with some location shooting (in the case of *Island of Terror* and *Night of the Big Heat*, both of which were photographed by Reg Wyer, some very picturesque location shooting). A key setting in all three films turns out to be the local pub. On very low-budget productions such as these, having a single set where all the principal characters can interact – rather than having these characters dispersed across several sets – obviously has budgetary advantages. But the solidity and attendant cosiness of these pub sets, and the sense we gain of them being separate from the real world outside, also helps to accentuate the way in which – particularly in *The Earth Dies Screaming* and *Night of the Big Heat* – they operate as refuges for the characters from an external alien threat. Throughout his career Fisher was primarily a studio-based director, and because of this his films often have an artificial quality to them. One thinks here, for example, of the swamp in *The Mummy* and the ruined abbey in *The Hound of the Baskervilles*; both are exterior settings but both were clearly shot in a studio, and arguably the films in which they appear benefit from a sense of their apart-ness from and strangeness in relation to the more quotidian exterior scenes that were shot on location. The three invasion films are different inasmuch as they have contemporary settings which lend themselves more to a surface realism, but even here one feels that a large part of the claustrophobia and isolation projected by these films – as well as the sense they give of a tension between the internal and the external – derives from Fisher's use of some confined, even theatrical, sets.

Of the three films, *The Earth Dies Screaming* is the most atmospheric. A mere 62 minutes in length – in this another throwback to Fisher's support-feature days – the film's narrative is told with commendable economy and efficiency. A handful of survivors from what appears to have been a gas attack (the extent of which remains unclear although it could be world-wide) meet up in a small village. There they encounter robot invaders who are eventually defeated when the transmission device that is guiding them is destroyed. As SF narratives go, this is a fairly conventional and formulaic one: the characters – including the resourceful male leader who states that everyone needs to co-operate, his cowardly opponent who retorts that 'It's every man for himself', the young married couple expecting a baby, the middle-aged couple – are all recognisable stereotypes who don't do anything that you don't expect them to do. The film's distinctiveness, such as it is, lies instead in the detail, in its eerie presentation of an idyllic village where dead bodies litter the streets and space-suited robots march past, in the scenes in which the dead villagers rise as mindless zombies, in the shock moment where someone sees a robot's impassive face for the first time (with the crudity of the special effects here bestowing upon the scene a certain primal force).

It is interesting to note the extent to which the scenario of *The Earth Dies Screaming* – an apparently extraterrestrial event kills people who then rise from the dead and threaten the living – anticipates the story for George Romero's important 1968 US horror film *The Night of the Living Dead*; and the style of *The Earth Dies Screaming* too – the stark black and white photography, an accompanying sense of mundane normality utterly overcome by an inexplicable alien threat – lends weight to such a comparison.

(Even Elisabeth Lutyens' musical score for Fisher's film is similar to the music used in *The Night of the Living Dead*.) The differences between the two films are important as well, of course. Romero's ruthless killing-off of every one of his characters would have been unthinkable for the more conventionally-minded Fisher, although the ending Fisher does provide is hardly an affirmative one. As his main characters (one of whom just happens to be a pilot) fly off into the distance, we – and so far as we know, they – have no sense of where they can go.[3] One should not make too much of this comparison, but given that Fisher's position in the history of horror is usually to be the exemplar of the conservative, patriarchal approach that is eventually displaced by the more socially critical post-1968 American horror film, it is significant that his work anticipates some of those later developments. It suggests that the history of horror is perhaps less straightforward than some accounts have made it out to be.

In comparison with *The Earth Dies Screaming*, *Island of Terror* and *Night of the Big Heat* are much more obviously horror-orientated projects. Filmed in colour, both feature horror star Peter Cushing while Christopher Lee shows up in *Night of the Big Heat*. Very little time in either is spent on an exploration of scientific concepts; instead the stress is on the violent assaults of non-human creatures upon small isolated communities. In *Island of Terror*, in particular, these assaults are surprisingly gruesome for a British film from the mid-1960s, with the monsters noisily sucking out the bones of their victims and leaving behind some decidedly floppy corpses. Some of the attitudes on display in *Island of Terror* are recognisable from Fisher's other work. Most notably, the community under threat turns out to be incapable of organising its own defence and consequently is in desperate need of leadership. This becomes strikingly apparent in the climactic scene when the community is trapped in a building where the power supply might fail. One of the community leaders, worried about the prospect of such a failure, comments of his charges, 'They're frightened without the light'. We are not a million miles away here from the fearful peasants in *Dracula*, *The Brides of Dracula* and *The Gorgon*. It is significant in this respect that in the only one of Fisher's pre-horror films that engages at any length with notions of community – the comedy *Children Galore* – the community in question is similarly disorganised, internally divided and child-like. It seems that throughout his career, Fisher was either unable or unwilling to present the community in a positive light, and this might help to explain his attraction to those charismatic authority figures who, in Hammer horror in particular, take charge.

In *Island of Terror*, two authority figures are imported from the mainland – doctors played by Peter Cushing and Edward Judd – who lead the fight against the monsters and whose authority is unquestioningly accepted by the grateful islanders. However, their authority turns out to be not nearly as boundless as that of the Hammer savant; not only does Cushing lose an arm to the monsters but, in the climactic siege, the prospect of defeat looms so large that Cushing and Judd prepare to kill Judd's girlfriend before the bone-sucking monsters can get to her. Fortunately – both for the girlfriend and the islanders – Cushing and Judd's strategy of feeding cattle infected with radioactive material to the monsters works, and at the last possible moment all the monsters die. Even with this success, the overwhelming sense one gains of the film's conclusion is of characters passively and helplessly waiting, with fingers crossed, for chance to intervene. This is hardly the Hammer way.

Similar elements – the isolated and divided community, a reliance on chance to defeat the invaders – are apparent in *Night of the Big Heat* which details the responses of various islanders and outsiders to an intense heatwave that presages an extraterrestrial invasion. While *The Earth Dies Screaming* and *Island of Terror* had generally viewed the invasion as a threat emanating from outside the community, the more interesting *Night of the Big Heat* explores in some detail (and far more forcefully than the 1959 John Lymington novel upon which the film was based) the ways in which the invasion not only exacerbates tensions within the community but also to a certain extent is an expression of those tensions. The rising heat on the island is shown to loosen civilised constraints and in particular unleash sexual drives.[4] This is most obviously represented by one of the islander's attempted rape of recently-arrived newcomer Angela as well as by Angela's own nymphomania. Here the heat outside parallels a sexual heat within; the film itself makes the connection between climate and sexuality when one of its characters, seeing Angela for the first time, remarks, 'No wonder the temperature's way up.' Sexuality emerges as a force that is itself alien, a force outside the conscious will, something that manages to be both internal and external. The view of sexuality thus offered resembles that found in Fisher's *Dracula*, with the sexual threat of the vampire outside the bedroom window corresponding to the sexual desire of the willing victim waiting for him in the bedroom, although *Night of the Big Heat* focuses far more than *Dracula* on female sexuality, especially as embodied by Angela.

Angela is one of two outsiders on the island; the other is a scientist (played by Christopher Lee). Both are associated with the extraterrestrials – the first time we hear the whining noise produced by the aliens is just as Angela arrives on the island; the scientist is seen emerging from one of the alien haunts on the island – and as in a sense aliens themselves on the small island they are both perceived as threats by the other characters. However, while Lee's scientist turns out to be working for the good of the islanders, Angela is a much harder figure to recuperate. An ex-lover of local pub landlord-cum-novelist Jeff Cullen, she has come to the island with the sole intention of breaking up Jeff's marriage. From the beginning she is clearly marked as an intruder – with her fast sports car and her sexual aggressiveness. The local doctor (played by Peter Cushing) describes her as 'quite the modern miss' while for a more blunt Jeff she is 'a slut' and for Jeff's wife she is a 'selfish bitch'. Unkind words perhaps, but the film itself appears to endorse them by having Angela act in a progressively cowardly, stupid, selfish and panic-stricken manner as the extraterrestrial threat escalates. Seen in this way, *Night of the Big Heat* stands as a warning against the dangers of an independent female sexuality and is comparable in these terms with some other horror films from the mid to late 1960s – including Fisher's own *Frankenstein Created Woman* along with John Gilling's *The Reptile* (1966) and Michael Reeves' *The Sorcerers* (1967) – which engaged with a similar theme and which seemed to function as somewhat anxious responses to a growing sexual permissiveness in British society.

As we will see, Fisher offered much more complex and less moralistic treatments of the independent women in his post-1962 work for Hammer, but *Night of the Big Heat* is interesting precisely because of its difference from that Hammer work. The lack of any savant figures – Lee's scientist does not possess the requisite authority – and the stress instead on the actions of 'normal' people is unusual for Fisher in this part of his career, and while the nymphomaniac Angela might be presented in a decidedly negative light, the men themselves hardly emerge as paragons of virtue. Not only do we have an attempted rapist on the island but Jeff, the film's ostensible hero, is an adulterer who seems incapable of resisting Angela's charms.[5] The end result is a sense of imperfection and emotional stasis, with characters unable to develop or move on. Appropriately for such a world, the aliens are not defeated by the intervention of humans but instead by a chance downpour of rain. On one level, this is a bathetic conclusion – the invasion is in effect rained off – but the very arbitrariness of this (and indeed the arbitrariness of the invasions in *The Earth Dies Screaming* and *Island of Terror*) highlights the ways in which these films, in their solidly English way, seem to belong to a more modern tradition of horror than that represented by Hammer horror. It is a type of horror that stresses the helplessness of its main characters and the inadequacy of social authority and it appears periodically throughout the 1960s in films such as *The Birds* (1963), *Night of the Living Dead* and *Rosemary's Baby* (1968) before reaching full fruition in the 1970s American horror film and in the British horror work of directors like Pete Walker and Norman J. Warren.[6] As was noted above, Fisher's horror films are often presented as antithetical to this type of horror, but here, in three films which ostensibly at least present themselves as science fiction, there seems to be a connection with an altogether more modern take on horror-related themes. Much the same can be said of the work Fisher was doing for Hammer in this period.

Female monsters

In *Our Vampires, Ourselves*, an impressive account of vampirism in literature and film, Nina Auerbach discusses the scene from Fisher's *Dracula* in which Lucy awaits Dracula's arrival in her bedroom: 'She removes her crucifix, lies down, and, in a tender rhythm of autoeroticism, fondles the vampire bites on her neck. We never see Christopher Lee enter her room; the sequence fades out on the open window. The scene suggests vampirism, but we see, instead, a woman alone, claiming herself.'[7] Auerbach also finds traces of autoeroticism – and an accompanying sense of women existing apart from or in resistance to male actions – in Mina's behaviour. While acknowledging that these elements of female 'independence' are ultimately contained by male authority, Auerbach finds these 'tantalizing images of transformation'[8] a significant part of *Dracula*'s appeal.

Such moments of female autonomy are clearly snatched from a film which elsewhere, and very systematically, privileges the exercise of male authority. The harsh treatment meted out to the likes of the villainous Cecile Stapleton in *The Hound of the Baskervilles* and 'modern miss' Angela Roberts in *Night of the Big Heat* suggests that Fisher's reputation as a male-centred, even chauvinistic, film-maker was well founded, and that those parts of *Dracula* valued by Auerbach are, in the context of Fisher's career as a whole, anomalous. However, so far as his post-*Phantom of the Opera* work for Hammer was concerned, it is fair to say that a change of attitude to women becomes apparent, with this also having implications for the ways in which masculinity and male authority are represented. As with *Night of the Big Heat*, this can be seen as anticipating a later more widespread questioning of social authority that develops in both American and British horror, most visibly throughout the 1970s, but it also has a particular resonance within Fisher's career. Fisher's films had occasionally in the past presented female heroes – notably in *So Long at the Fair* and *The Brides of Dracula* – although the activities of these figures had always been curtailed by the intervention of men – by the artist played by Dirk Bogarde in *So Long at the Fair* and by Van Helsing in *The Brides of Dracula*. In Fisher's later, post-1962 Hammer work, one finds not only a greater uncertainty about where to place the limits of female agency but also, importantly, a greater awareness of the authoritative nature of the interchange between men and women in the Hammer horror world. As is always the case in Fisher's career, there is no sense that he initiated this change himself. It is more a case of Fisher beginning to respond in a particular way to the scenarios given him by Hammer. That this response tends to be couched in terms of male anxiety and male fear is perhaps not surprising given Fisher's previous attachment to masculine themes and issues, but nevertheless it does seem that some of the possibilities for autonomous female representation found by Nina Auerbach in *Dracula* become a more developed feature of Fisher's work in this period.

A shift of focus is certainly evident in *The Gorgon*, Fisher's 'come-back' film for Hammer. Scripted by John Gilling from a story by John Llewellyn Devine (and, like *The Brides of Dracula*, revised by an uncredited Anthony Hinds), it was the first Hammer horror to centre on a female monster. Of course, there had been female monsters and femme fatales in earlier Hammers – one thinks of the vampire women and Lucy in *Dracula* and of Cecile Stapleton in *The Hound of the Baskervilles* – but these had always been subordinated to a dominant male. *The Gorgon* contains no such dominant male but offers instead a veritable procession of weak or defeated men, including three figures – Professor Heitz (played by Michael Gwynne), Dr Namaroff (Peter Cushing) and Professor Meister (Christopher Lee) – of the right age and stature (and gender) to be Hammer savants. (As if to underline this, Meister is the German word for 'master'.) Of these three, the first two turn out to be less than adequate and are killed by the Gorgon while the more effective Meister manages to kill the Gorgon but fails to save the young Paul Heitz whom he has tried to protect.

The female monster in question is Megaera, who, according to the film, was one of the three Gorgons. (In fact – or in mythology – Megaera was actually one of the Furies or Eumenides rather than one of the Gorgons. It seems that a knowledge of Greek mythology was not one of Hammer's strong points.) This monster has in some unspecified way possessed Carla, a nurse at Dr Namaroff's Institute. We have already seen how a number of Fisher's earlier films were structured around a series of doublings, and here we have another significant doubling relationship – this time between Carla and Megaera. Of the two, Carla (played by Barbara Shelley) is the 'good', compliant one, respectful of male authority and generally doing what men tell her to do. She is associated with the Institute which is presented by Fisher as a space ruled over by men, notably Namaroff, that imprisons women, most obviously the madwoman whom Namaroff is studying but also Carla herself. By contrast, Megaera (played by Prudence Hyman), is associated with the apparently abandoned and disused Castle Borski, a space linked with female mastery and male death – Professor Heitz, his son Paul Heitz and Dr Namaroff all receive their fatal exposure to the Gorgon within its walls. The film as a whole deals with the inability of various men to control Carla, to free her from the influence of Megaera and the castle. The loss of male authority this involves is signalled most particularly through the weakening of the male gaze. To look at the Gorgon is to die, and the film is replete with images of men screaming at the sight of Megaera. It is actually quite rare to find a horror film that relies as extensively on the representation of male fear as does *The Gorgon*, and Fisher illustrates male subjection as skilfully as elsewhere in his work he does male authority. For example, Professor Heitz's entrance into the castle repeats the track/pan technique used for Jonathan Harker's entrance into Castle Dracula in *Dracula*, but Heitz's movements are much more tentative and hesitant than Harker's and the camera movement itself slower, less forceful. Later scenes in which Paul Heitz enters the castle to find Carla seated regally on a throne and, on his second visit, Dr Namaroff waiting to kill him enhance a sense of the castle as a space separate from the male-run police state of Vandorf in which the film takes place, a space which reveals a truth inexpressible elsewhere – namely, Carla's power as she looks down on Paul, and Namaroff's weakness as he wields a large and decidedly phallic sword to rid himself of a rival for Carla's attentions.

Of course, focusing on the weakness of men does not automatically lead to the production of the 'positive' images of women that Nina Auerbach found intermittently expressed in *Dracula*. Indeed, for all the threat she represents to men, the Gorgon is a monster defined entirely in terms of her relation to the male gaze. Men look at her and then they die: she does not do anything to cause this, she just is.[9] That Carla herself seems to have no conscious awareness of her 'Gorgon side', as well as the fact that Carla and the Gorgon are played by different actresses, forestalls any detailed exploration of the transformative possibilities of this particular doubling relationship. It is significant in this respect that the film contains no transformation scene showing us Carla turning into the Gorgon, merely a brief sequence at the end where Megaera's severed head turns back into Carla's head.[10] Other of the film's shortcomings include a screenplay with more than its fair share of improbabilities and loose ends and, most of all, the visualisation of Megaera herself. Cinema has never managed a convincing portrayal of the Gorgon, but of all the attempts to do so – notably in *The Seven Faces of Dr Lao* (1964) and *Clash of the Titans* (1981) – Hammer's is by far the least impressive. A desperately cheap-looking set of plastic snakes sits uneasily on the head of an unfortunate actress. Fisher had always made a point of placing his monsters clearly in the frame, but in this case keeping the monster in the shadows would probably have been more effective (and would have fitted in with the strategy he uses generally in *The Gorgon* of having characters emerging quietly from or disappearing into a shadowy background).

In clarifying what (for all its shortcomings) is significant and valuable about *The Gorgon*, it is useful to compare it with another Hammer female-monster movie, *The Reptile*, directed in 1966 by John Gilling who had also received the main screenwriting credit for *The Gorgon* (although Gilling had apparently disowned the project after his script was revised by Anthony Hinds).[11] Both *The Gorgon* and *The Reptile* are female-transformation stories: Carla turns into Megaera, Anna in *The Reptile* becomes, as one might expect, a large reptile. So far as the visual presentation of the monster is concerned, *The Reptile* improves considerably upon its predecessor. The reptile herself is a genuinely frightening creature, far from the unconvincing apparition that is Megaera; and stylistically, too, Gilling brings a freshness and spontaneity to the proceedings that is generally lacking from Fisher's more obviously studio-bound film.

Having said this, *The Gorgon* is conceptually much more daring than *The Reptile* which, for all the skill with which it is made, tends simply to reproduce the by now highly standardised Hammer horror formula. So in *The Reptile* the evil emanates from a foreign land and is ultimately defeated by an English soldier-hero who might lack the detailed technical knowledge of a savant but more than makes up for this deficiency by his propensity for action; and, as expected, the normative heterosexual couple survive while all the deviant people die. As we have already seen, *The Gorgon* refuses such a straightforward and affirmative scenario, and Fisher's mise-en-scene is perfectly suited to conveying the film's relentlessly masochistic theme. This is particularly apparent in his treatment of Castle Borski. Here a meticulous deployment of space – with the powerful Megaera associated with the castle's upper reaches while the lowly men belong to the ground floor – and attention to detail in the castle's décor – with Megaera's victims all reflected in a mirror before or just after they face their doom – transform the castle into something more than just the physical location of the monster. The repeated visits of men to the castle imply a male obsession, a masochistic compulsion to look even if death results, and as the site of this compulsion the castle arguably comes to function, for all its solidity, as an expression of that fearful male psychological state – with the Gorgon herself marked as a projection of an inner male anxiety (hence the mirror in which men are reflected before they become her victims). *The Reptile,* too, uses repetition. The film begins with a man venturing into a house and proceeding down a corridor, at the end of which he is attacked by the reptile. Later in the film the man's brother walks down the same corridor and is attacked by the reptile in exactly the same way. But here the repetition simply serves the mechanics of suspense – we have seen what happened once in this corridor and we fear that it will happen again – and it entirely lacks the unsettling uncanny dimension one finds in *The Gorgon.*

Seen in this way, Fisher's film is one of his most dream-like projects. The landscape itself becomes psychologically charged in a drama in which masculinity is repeatedly assaulted by an overwhelming sense of female otherness but where – as if to underline the film's male-centredness – the real woman, Carla, plays very little part in the action. At the very end of the film, in a scene that is comparable with the scene in *Dracula* where Arthur looks at Lucy after she has been staked, Paul Heitz looks at the Gorgon's severed head and sees it transformed back into Carla's head. In both cases, the weakened male gaze – Arthur's and Paul's – is thereby restored, but with the difference that in *The Gorgon* most of the men are dead and Paul himself dying. This is a hollow victory indeed, and a final reminder of the male inadequacy around which the film has been structured.

After the decidedly outré outing that was *The Gorgon*, Fisher's next film for Hammer seemed a return to more traditional fare. *Dracula – Prince of Darkness* marked Christopher Lee's return to the role of Count Dracula. As was the case with *The Brides of Dracula*, this sequel to the original *Dracula* afforded Fisher the opportunity to go back over material he had already covered, developing, elaborating, revising. The principal difference between *The Brides of Dracula* and *Dracula – Prince of Darkness* is that while the former was, in terms of its story at least, a bit of a mess, *Dracula – Prince of Darkness* (as written by Jimmy Sangster, himself making a comeback to Hammer period horror under the pseudonym John Sansom) offered instead a minimal, stripped down version of the Hammer formula. The very simple story proceeds as follows. Two English couples holidaying in Transylvania wander into Castle Dracula where they encounter the sinister manservant Klove. During the night one of the Englishmen is murdered by Klove and his blood used to resurrect Dracula. The Count then vampirises the dead man's wife. The other couple escape and under the direction of a local monk they manage to destroy the vampire and his minions.

Perhaps the most striking feature of *Dracula – Prince of Darkness* is that it keeps us waiting so long for Dracula. The Count does appear in the pre-credits sequence which reprises the conclusion of *Dracula*, but thereafter he is absent from the screen for the first half of the film which focuses instead on the exploits of the English tourists. So far as its function within the narrative is concerned, the couples' naïve, unsuspecting encounter with vampirism is comparable with Marianne's experiences at the Castle Meinster in *The Brides of Dracula*. In both films, the disparity between our knowledge of the vampire and the characters' knowledge generates suspense – when will they find out? – and satisfaction – at last! they have found out. There is something very schematic about this part of *Dracula – Prince of Darkness*. The two couples have obviously been designed to be contrasted with each other: Charles and Diana are the 'normal' couple who survive Dracula while Alan and Helen are the problematic couple – with the husband hen-pecked and the wife emotionally repressed – who die in the course of the film.[12] In addition, the two couples' ignorance of vampires stands in stark opposition to the knowledge and wisdom of the film's savant-authority figure, Father Sandor.

There is not much room for ambiguity here (although, as we will see, there is some room) and Fisher does not even try to subvert this very formulaic scenario but instead uses it as the basis for some bravura camerawork. As David Pirie has noted: 'Fisher allows his camera to prowl around the deserted castle in a series of movements which evoke with a poetic grandeur the unseen presence of the departed host.'[13] Fisher is also alert to the fact that even by the usual standards of the vampire film, his two English couples are particularly slow on the uptake when it comes to spotting that they have wandered into a vampire's house. The director compensates by embracing some of the comic possibilities of the scenario although as usual he never allows this to degenerate into broad humour. So lines such as Klove's 'My master died without issue, sir, in the accepted sense of the term', which clearly have a double meaning with one of those meanings passing completely over the heads of the unsuspecting visitors to Castle Dracula, are delivered (and filmed) straight and, arguably, are all the more effective for that. There is also something potentially humorous, or at the very least incongruous, about Alan's death – not in the graphic details of his being stabbed, suspended upside down from the ceiling and then having his throat cut but rather in the fact that this sort of thing could happen to a respectable Englishman wandering through a castle in his dressing gown and slippers. Again the incongruity is not stressed but is clearly there as a background element.

Ironically, things start to go wrong with *Dracula – Prince of Darkness* once Dracula has been resurrected for it quickly becomes clear that the film is not entirely sure what to do with him. We see a lot of vampiric posturing and snarling (this is the Dracula film where Dracula himself has no dialogue) but Dracula's motivation – apparently his desire to claim Diana – seems petty and his powers rather limited for someone who is meant to be Lord of the Undead. Fisher's first Dracula film had avoided posing the question 'What does Dracula want?' by keeping the vampire off-screen for much of the film and making Van Helsing instead the dramatic centre of interest.[14] *Dracula – Prince of Darkness* reveals all too clearly a lack of clarity about Dracula and in so doing anticipates the increasingly marginal nature of the character in Hammer's later Dracula films (none of which would be directed by Fisher).

Significantly in this respect, the most interesting character in *Dracula – Prince of Darkness* turns out to be not Count Dracula (nor for that matter Father Sandor) but instead Helen Kent, wife of the unfortunate Alan. On one level, her transformation from emotionally repressed English woman to wanton vampire is just as schematic as the rest of the film, but, thanks largely to Fisher's direction and Barbara Shelley's performance, Helen becomes both unexpectedly nuanced and a focus for some interesting ambiguities. She is clearly more complex than her travelling companions and does not share their complacency about the foreign land through which they are all travelling. While her primness is initially off-putting, the fact that she is the only one of them who does not want to enter Castle Dracula demonstrates that her perceptions, for all their intuitive nature, are well founded.

Helen first appears as a vampire to Diana, Charles' wife. 'Come sister, you don't need Charles', she says as she advances with fangs bared on Diana. The line is both intriguing and ambiguous. Could it mean – you don't need Charles, you need Dracula? Given that Dracula promptly appears and drags Diana away from Helen, it seems unlikely that Helen is here acting on the Count's behalf. Does the line then mean – you don't need Charles, you need me? Again unlikely; at no other point does the film even hint at lesbianism.[15] Or what about – you don't need Charles, or any other man for that matter? This is the interpretation favoured by Nina Auerbach in *Our Vampires, Ourselves* who sees Helen's 'wicked remark' as undermining male authority and provoking the wrath of Dracula and Charles, both of whom immediately enter the scene and separate the two women: 'The forces of darkness and light converge against the vampire who told the woman that she didn't need her man.'[16]

Operating as a counterpoint to what is, potentially at least, an assertion of female autonomy is the most discussed scene in *Dracula – Prince of Darkness* – the staking of the vampiric Helen by Father Sandor. Trapped in a monastery, she is held down on a table by a group of monks while Sandor administers the fatal stake. S. S. Prawer, *Dracula – Prince of Darkness*'s sternest critic, has described the scene thus: 'What it shows in fact is figures in the garb of sanctity performing an obscene parody of a gang-rape that ends with murder.'[17] Nina Auerbach discusses the scene in a similar way: 'The sequence is closer to gang rape, or to gynecological (sic) surgery, or to any of the collective violations women were and are prone to, than to the sacred marriage Stoker's reverent narrators made readers accept ... the staking of the female vampire is less a rite of purification than the licensed torture of a woman who knew women didn't need men.'[18]

'Gang rape', 'torture': these are shocking, emotive terms, especially when deployed in relation to a scene which, ostensibly at least, shows the triumph of good over evil. Undoubtedly the scene is very powerful and, like other stakings in Fisher's films, contains a sexual component. Whether this can legitimately be interpreted as, in effect, a rape scene is another matter, however. It can be argued that there is a rush to judgement apparent in Prawer's and Auerbach's accounts of the sequence, with this involving a premature abandonment of its *literal* meaning in favour of what is seen as the true *figurative* meaning. As Prawer notes, the staking of Helen needs to be contrasted with *Dracula – Prince of Darkness*'s opening sequence which shows Father Sandor preventing some fearful villagers (all of them men) from staking the dead body of a young woman in the mistaken belief that she is a vampire. Sandor's intervention establishes him as the knowledgeable figure of authority, the film's savant. The staking of Helen thus becomes an expression of the authority and expertise which the villagers themselves conspicuously lack.

But the other comparison that can profitably be made here is with Van Helsing's staking of Lucy in Fisher's *Dracula*. It clearly serves an identical function to the Helen scene – in each a wayward woman is put back into her 'proper', socially sanctioned place (at the cost of her life) – but the differences are instructive. Lucy's staking is achieved quite easily. She sleeps in her coffin while Van Helsing, the man with the requisite knowledge of vampires, dispatches her in a dispassionate manner. Helen does not go as easily. She is awake, and the monks can only hold her down with considerable effort. To a certain extent, this difference depends on the actresses involved: Barbara Shelley is much more physically imposing than the gamine Carol Marsh who plays Lucy. (As Auerbach puts it, 'Barbara Shelley is large and strong.'[19]) In addition, Fisher's handling of the scene stresses Helen's resistance as much as it does Sandor's authority. It seems from this that the film's depiction of the staking of Helen is not merely about the assertion of a savant's authority but also about how difficult such an assertion has become. In this, *Dracula – Prince of Darkness* is comparable with *The Gorgon*. While neither is overtly critical of the authority of the male savant, both of them do register a significant female resistance to that authority. Ultimately, of course, the savant wins through – albeit in Pyrrhic fashion in *The Gorgon* – but in any event one definitely gains a sense of a change taking place in Fisher's work, of the beginnings of a move away from the certainties of, say, *Dracula* or *The Revenge of Frankenstein*. In Fisher's remaining films for Hammer, these changes would be manifested more clearly and more self-consciously.

The Baron and the Devil

David Pirie has observed that British horror cinema had by 1966 'lost some of its original rigidity and was beginning to hunt for new talent and new ideas'.[20] In particular, the brilliant young director Michael Reeves was about to introduce both a psychological intensity and an emphasis on youth that had largely been lacking in earlier British horror films. Usually Fisher is seen as a figure existing apart from this new, exciting activity. There is a sense in which by the mid-1960s he had become the grand old man of British horror, the main representative of a conservative and moralistic tradition against which the daring and radical approaches of film-makers like Reeves in the 1960s and Gary Sherman and Pete Walker in the 1970s were a kind of reaction. As accounts of British horror go, this is too simplistic. For one thing, the work of these younger directors was more conservative in certain respects than it might at first appear (with this particularly the case for Reeves and Walker). For another, Fisher's horror work was not straightforwardly conservative. This has already been noted in relation to his earlier horror films – in which a privileging of authority is always intertwined with a fascination with weakness and subjection – but it is even more apparent in the four films he makes for Hammer after Dracula – Prince of Darkness – namely Frankenstein Created Woman, The Devil Rides Out, Frankenstein Must Be Destroyed and Frankenstein and the Monster from Hell. With these films, Fisher reveals himself as a film-maker as much caught up in and a part of broader changes in British horror as other younger film-makers.

Frankenstein Created Woman was the fourth of Hammer's seven Frankenstein films. The first two of these – The Curse of Frankenstein and The Revenge of Frankenstein – had, of course, been directed by Fisher. The third, The Evil of Frankenstein (1964), directed by Freddie Francis, was a decidedly lacklustre affair that unwisely returned to the idea of the mute, mindless monster found in The Curse of Frankenstein and some of the lesser Universal horror films from the 1930s and 1940s, an idea comprehensively abandoned in the more subtle The Revenge of Frankenstein. As would be the case later with *Frankenstein Must Be Destroyed* and *Frankenstein and the Monster from Hell*, Fisher reworks elements from *The Revenge of Frankenstein* in *Frankenstein Created Woman*, particularly the intertwining of the contrasted stories of Frankenstein's mastery and his creation's subjection. He is aided in this by the simple, linear story provided for him by screenwriter Anthony Hinds (in his John Elder persona) which, as with *Dracula – Prince of Darkness*, affords him opportunities to refine and add nuance and complexity to what were by now familiar and well-established characters and situations.

The story of *Frankenstein Created Woman* is as follows. Hans, who is one of Frankenstein's assistants, is executed for a murder which he did not commit; Christina, his distraught girlfriend, then kills herself. Frankenstein transplants the soul of the assistant into the dead woman's body. The resurrected Christina then tracks down and kills the three young men actually responsible for the murder of which Hans was unjustly accused. Frankenstein himself is unable to prevent the deaths of the three men and looks on helplessly as his female 'creation' commits suicide at the end of the film. As before, the three principal elements here are Frankenstein, the creature and the society in which the action takes place; but in each of these, and in their interrelation, one sees significant changes from their relatively straightforward deployment in the earlier *The Revenge of Frankenstein*.

The Baron, for example, is altogether more benign than he was in previous films. Grey-haired and frailer looking than before, he does not kill anyone and seems to have dispensed with his gorier experiments in favour of the study of the human soul. He still possesses an arrogant sense of his own superiority – as is demonstrated in the trial scene when the prosecutor sarcastically remarks 'You're a very clever man then, Baron' and the Baron matter-of-factly replies 'Yes, I am' – but not to the extent that he becomes a dangerously anti-social figure. Indeed, this is the only one of Fisher's Frankenstein films other than *The Curse of Frankenstein* where the Baron is not obliged to conceal his identity but instead lives openly in the community, albeit on its margins.

The community itself is presented in a less negative light than in *The Revenge of Frankenstein* where the hypocrisy and closed-mindedness of the medical council provides a stark counterpoint to the truth-seeking activities of the Baron. Certainly Fisher identifies a harsh and judgemental element in the society he presents in *Frankenstein Created Woman*: the first image in the film is a low-angle shot of the guillotine that stands on the edge of the town as a reminder of an inflexible system of justice, and the opening sequence depicts an execution where the liveliness of the condemned man is used to underline the awfulness of the execution procedure. (One might compare this with the Baron's 'execution' in *The Revenge of Frankenstein* which is played for blackly comic effect.) Elsewhere in the film, however, this harshness is ameliorated, notably in the set-piece trial scene where the cruel prosecutor is contrasted with the judge who makes every effort to ensure that justice is done and clearly regrets having to pass the death sentence. In effect, we have three different attitudes represented in the trial: the aloof superiority of the Baron (who is first glimpsed idly thumbing through a Bible, as if searching for loopholes), the inflexibility of the prosecutor, and the humanity of the judge, with all of these seen as inadequate in some way or other. Both the Baron and the prosecutor are indifferent to the fate of Hans, while the judge, for all his compassion, is unable to save the accused.

This complicating of what in *The Revenge of Frankenstein* had been schematic oppositions is carried over into *Frankenstein Created Woman*'s treatment of its 'monster'. Christina is the daughter of the local inn-keeper; scarred and lame, she is a figure of fun for the three young men who end up drunkenly killing her father. After her suicide, she is resurrected by Frankenstein as a beautiful blonde killing machine who does in her father's killers then commits suicide for a second time. She is the third successive female monster for Fisher – after Megaera in *The Gorgon* and Helen in *Dracula – Prince of Darkness* – but the nature of her monstrousness is quite different. As with Karl in *The Revenge of Frankenstein*, she is presented so sympathetically that it seems unfair to think of her as a monster (although she does do some monstrous things), and, again as with Karl, there is a focus on the problematic nature of her identity. Christina's first words after being resurrected are 'Who am I?' but just before her (second) suicide she tells Frankenstein 'I know who I am'; and it is in the passage between these two statements that Fisher explores the whole question of who Christina really is and the implications this has for our understanding of Frankenstein.

The scenario envisaged by *Frankenstein Created Woman* of a male soul inhabiting a female body is undeniably perverse. David Pirie has described Christina's resurrection as 'an utterly sensual, hermaphroditic and polymorphous-perverse rejuvenation'.[21] However, the film does not exploit this as much as it might have. In particular it avoids the possibilities for same-sex desire raised by the very idea of a man in a female body luring other men to their deaths with the promise of sex, and it does this by presenting Hans' presence in Christina as a sporadic possession rather than as a full-time occupancy. The post-operative Christina therefore oscillates between periods of apparent self-control and periods when she is controlled by Hans whose influence is thereby signalled as external to her, as an unnatural imposition from elsewhere.[22] According to Pirie, 'Christina stalks and lures her victims with a kind of vampiric power continually acting out the fears of all sexual fantasy by metamorphosing into a vengeful beast at the moment of intercourse.'[23] It appears that she is the Lamia, the embodiment of all male fears. What Pirie neglects to mention is that the killings are the moments where Hans is most obviously in charge of Christina, where in a sense Christina herself is absent. (While Christina does have a motive for revenge, it is clearly Hans' need for vengeance that motivates the killings.)

Fisher's staging of the killings is interesting in this respect. With each of them, Christina initially appears to the three men – Anton, Karl and Johann – in the guise of a seductress, quite unlike the manner she adopts with Frankenstein (or with anyone else in the film for that matter). In the case of both Anton and Karl, she then leaves them – 'To change', she explains to Anton – and waits for them to follow her; with Anton she disappears behind a curtain while with Karl she stands patiently in a pool of shadow. After this dramatic pause, we – and the potential victims – then hear Hans' voice, although, as we do not see Christina speaking, Hans himself remains a spectral, disembodied presence. There is something very theatrical about all of this, a strong sense of Christina – under the control of Hans – performing a role, the role of the deadly woman, for the benefit of a male audience (i.e. the victims). In effect, what we have here is a male (Hans') drama-tisation of male desires and male fears about women, in which Christina herself is merely a vessel for the expression of those desires and fears.

At the end of the film, having killed her three men, Christina stands on the edge of a river bank. The Baron tries to dissuade her from suicide. 'Let me tell you who you really are', he says (some-what belatedly). 'I know who I am, of what I have to do. Forgive me', Christina replies and throws herself into the river. The Baron looks on helplessly and then walks away, and the film ends. This is the moment that *The Gorgon* lacked. Lurking in that film, although never made explicit, was a sense that Megaera was a summation of essentially male fears and anxieties and that she only really existed in relation to a male-centred view of the world: she had no voice of her own, all she could do was provoke a male reaction. In contrast, *Frankenstein Created Woman* concludes with a female refusal, Christina's refusal, to allow the Baron to define her identity. It is hardly an affirmative ending – Christina dies after all – but it is striking for the explicit way in which it places limitations on Frankenstein's authority. He cannot control her nor can he speak for her; finally, she speaks for herself.

If *Frankenstein Created Woman* traces a decline in male authority, Fisher's next film for Hammer, *The Devil Rides Out*, seems to reinstate that authority in very emphatic terms. A tale of black magic based on Dennis Wheatley's best-selling novel, it sets up an opposition between two strong male authority figures (the good Duc de Richleau – played by Christopher Lee – and the evil Mocata – played by Charles Gray) in a manner comparable with *Dracula* (where it is Van Helsing versus Dracula) and *Dracula – Prince of Darkness* (Father Sandor versus Dracula). As with *Dracula* and *Dracula – Prince of Darkness*, caught between these two men are a range of younger characters who turn out to be incapable of defending themselves from evil and in order to survive have to put their faith in and obey the good authoritative figure, he who possesses the requisite knowledge of magic: in *The Devil Rides Out*, these people in need of help include Richleau's friend Rex, the ingenue Tanith and Simon Aaron as well as the married couple Richard and Marie. The quasi-paternalistic nature of the relationship between the savants and the 'normals' is most apparent in the way that both De Richleau and Mocata treat Simon. 'I feel like a father who sees his child trying to pick live coals out of a fire', De Richleau remarks on discovering Simon's involvement with black magic; 'Welcome back, my son', says Mocata when Simon returns to the coven. As is so often the case in Fisher's work, the good father and the bad father co-exist, mutually defining, the authority they embody ultimately (and even with the climactic death of Mocata) viewed as indispensable.

The clarity of this scenario affords Fisher the opportunity to do what he does best – to visualise authority and subjection, both in isolation from each other and in interaction. In fact, *The Devil Rides Out* turns out to be one of Fisher's most impressive films so far as its mise-en-scene is concerned. Horror historian David Pirie has already offered a masterly analysis of one of *The Devil Rides Out*'s most striking sequences – Mocata's hypnotising Marie in an attempt to reclaim Simon from the forces of good. Pirie convincingly demonstrates how the sequence is built upon a very precise and symmetrical pattern of editing; as before in his directorial career Fisher's background as an editor influences the way in which he shoots a scene.[24] The balance and order of Fisher's approach helps to stress the surface mundaneness of the sequence – which takes place in broad daylight – while the slow (to the point of being nearly imperceptible) forward camera movements that begin to appear as Mocata's influence takes hold give a strong sense of something evil stealthily invading this ordered world. Once the hypnosis is complete, Fisher cuts to a high angle shot of Mocata who looks up towards the camera. There follow cuts to various events taking place upstairs in the house, all of them caused by Mocata's will. After the balance of the first part of the sequence, this high angle shot marks the moment of Mocata's triumph, the moment when the insidious insertion of his will into Marie's home becomes an overt assault. And all of this is done visually – Mocata's monologue is unusually articulate for a Hammer film but it operates only as a minor counterpoint to Fisher's mise-en-scene.

Further instances from *The Devil Rides Out* of camera set-ups and movements demonstrating considerable skill and judgement are too numerous to list exhaustively, but what links them all together is their unobtrusive, self-effacing quality. They are not there to draw the attentions of the audience or critics to Fisher's artistry (and in this they were successful: *The Devil Rides Out* was widely ignored by critics on its initial release). Instead they service the narrative, convey atmosphere and also communicate an attitude to the events of and participants in the drama. Like most of Fisher's films, *The Devil Rides Out* operates on two levels. On the one hand, it is a very modest enterprise, content to tell its story in an unfussy way. On the other hand, its artifice and technique are in places remarkably complex and it displays a strong commitment throughout to telling the story cinematically, and in doing this exploiting to the full all the resources of cinema.

Take, for example, the sequence near the beginning of the film that shows De Richleau and Rex infiltrating a meeting of Mocata's coven. When De Richleau realises that they are about to be ejected, he moves amongst the members of the coven, listening in to their conversations. It's a fairly low-key moment in the film and, at first glance at least, seems visually less interesting than the later and more striking Mocata-hypnosis sequence. The first thing to say about Fisher's handling of the scene, however, is that he avoids some of the more obvious and conventional ways of filming it – cutting, perhaps, between De Richleau and the people coming to eject him from the meeting as a way of generating suspense. Instead De Richleau's eavesdropping is presented in the form of an elegant long take, with the camera slowly tracking backwards as well as panning on De Richleau's movement from one side of the room to another. The shot conveys very economically both De Richleau's purposeful authority – it is his movement which cues the camera's movements – and his affected casualness as he edges from one conversation to another. Operating as sinister counterpoint within the shot to De Richleau's inquisitive forward movement is Mocata's sudden appearance in the background staring suspiciously at De Richleau. Near the end of the shot De Richleau turns to face Mocata and, one presumes, there is a brief exchange of looks between them before De Richleau walks out of the shot. One has to presume this because there is no close-up of De Richleau's face at this moment; instead all we can see is the back of De Richleau's head (and in any event Mocata is so far away from the camera that it is hard to make out the details of his face). The deliberate withholding here of what by any accounts is a dramatic moment – the first signs of conflict between the film's principal hero and villain – helps to preserve the carefully considered rhythm of the sequence. As with the hypnosis sequence discussed by Pirie, an apparently innocuous scene – here a social gathering – is gradually disturbed by sinister undercurrents, culminating in an eruption of violence – here De Richleau's eventual abduction of Simon. Cutting in to and thereby highlighting a dramatically charged exchange of looks between De Richleau and Mocata would have interrupted this measured development, providing a short-term frisson at the expense of the effectiveness of the sequence as a whole. Instead Fisher's mise-en-scene positions the exchange of looks as a disturbing event but disturbing only in a muted, almost subliminal way.

The strategic and disciplined approach apparent here and elsewhere in *The Devil Rides Out* is aided immeasurably by the film's screenplay which was arguably the best Fisher ever had to work with. An earlier screenplay by John Hunter had been rejected by Hammer who had subsequently turned to Richard Matheson, noted American author of fantasy and horror tales. An earlier Hammer collaboration with Matheson in the late 1950s, an adaptation of his vampire novel *I Am Legend*, had been abandoned largely because of the British film censor's resistance to the project (although in 1965 Matheson had gone on to write for Hammer the screenplay for *Fanatic*, one of the studio's better psychological thrillers).[25] On this occasion, however, Matheson did a magnificent job of translating Dennis Wheatley's sprawling and verbose novel into a stream-lined, event-strewn narrative. Having said this, Matheson seems to have approached the adaptation in a fairly impersonal, workmanlike fashion, and the film betrays no obvious (or, for that matter, obscure) connections with his own very distinctive literary work – which included not only *I Am Legend*, indisputably one of the great vampire novels of the twentieth century, but also *The Shrinking Man* (filmed as *The Incredible Shrinking Man* by Jack Arnold in 1957 with a screenplay by Matheson himself).[26] Indeed, in a letter to Dennis Wheatley written after the release of *The Devil Rides Out*, Matheson seems to confirm his own self-effacing approach: 'I have written several novels myself and had their film versions murdered by scriptwriters; so when I became a scriptwriter myself, I swore that I would never mess up another author's story.'[27]

What Matheson's screenplay gave Fisher was a structure in which the lines of dramatic conflict were very clearly set out, with this in turn facilitating the measured directorial approach that characterises both the hypnosis scene and the 'coven' scene discussed above. Throughout the film as a whole, there is a sense therefore of clarity, of every element being in its right place. Memorable sequences function here not as isolated set-pieces (as was sometimes the case with striking sequences in Fisher's earlier films) but instead as part of a broader narrative pattern, one which constantly juxtaposes moments of brooding claustrophobic stillness – for instance, the sequence in the pentacle where De Richleau and his friends resist Mocata's magic – with expansive action scenes such as the one where De Richleau and Rex drive a car at speed into an open-air Sabbat.

The film even manages to incorporate an acknowledgement of female autonomy near the end, when it is Peggy, the daughter of Marie and Richard, rather than De Richleau who speaks the words of the magic ritual that finally defeats Mocata. Peggy is prompted in this by Marie who in turn has been temporarily possessed by the spirit of the dead (but soon to be resurrected) Tanith. There is a distinct resemblance between this moment and the climax of *Dracula – Prince of Darkness* inasmuch as both offer instances of unexpected female intervention and action. In the case of *Dracula*

– *Prince of Darkness*, it is Diana, exasperated by Father Sandor's apparent inability to save her husband from Dracula, who uses the rifle on the Count, thus giving Sandor the idea of how to destroy him (by shooting through the ice upon which the Count is standing and causing him to drown). Similarly, Marie, distraught over De Richleau's apparent unwillingness to save Peggy by repeating the words of a ritual used earlier to defeat the Angel of Death, intervenes herself (with the help of Tanith). In *Dracula – Prince of Darkness*, however, Diana is a thoroughly insipid character (unlike her sister-in-law Helen) and it seems that her actions at the end of the film are merely there to prompt Father Sandor into action. In the more complexly structured *The Devil Rides Out*, the intervention of the three women – Marie, Tanith and Peggy – takes place in a sequence which is almost immediately erased. The words of the ritual cause time to reverse and the film accordingly returns to an earlier point in the narrative and concludes with Tanith alive and the forces of good victorious. This structure, which separates out the scenes of female agency from the rest of the film, enables Fisher to preserve the authority of De Richleau so at the end of the film Tanith and Rex can appear hand in hand from the woods under his approving gaze. This is a world away from the conclusion of Fisher's previous film, *Frankenstein Created Woman* where the young person, Christina, absents herself from Frankenstein's controlling gaze by throwing herself into the river. Tensions which in *Frankenstein Created Woman* – and to a certain extent in *The Gorgon* and *Dracula – Prince of Darkness* – caused the hollowing out and partial collapse of male authority are in *The Devil Rides Out* held in balance, with this permitting the simultaneous affirmation both of male authority and of female autonomy; and it is a balance that is conveyed most effectively by Fisher's precise and finely judged mise-en-scene.

'I thought the world had seen the last of you': thus speaks Karl, a young doctor, on discovering that the man who has been blackmailing him is in fact the infamous Baron Frankenstein. *Frankenstein Must Be Destroyed*, the film in which this remark occurs, was the fifth in Hammer's Frankenstein series as well as Fisher's penultimate film. Even more than was the case with its predecessor in the series, *Frankenstein Created Woman*, it harked back to and reworked *The Revenge of Frankenstein*. Again we have an anti-social Baron forced to disguise himself, again we have a 'monster' (like the monster in *The Revenge of Frankenstein* the result of a brain transplant) characterised by his humanity and his suffering. By this stage, it is a well-rehearsed formula, and the Hammer film-makers – notable amongst them Fisher – play variations on it with a considerable facility.

However, the context in which these variations are worked out is not perhaps as clearly structured as it was with Fisher's previous film, *The Devil Rides Out*. In large part, this is to do with the script for *Frankenstein Must be Destroyed* which was not written by a seasoned professional writer of the likes of Richard Matheson but instead by Bert Batt who up until then was better known as an assistant director on numerous Hammer horrors.[28] The narrative he provides proves to be both simple (to the point of being minimal) and in places rather confused. For instance, a police inspector (played by Thorley Walters who had been Frankenstein's assistant in *Frankenstein Created Woman*) wanders in and out of the film to little apparent purpose, and the concluding scenes are overly reliant on various characters just happening to be in the same place at the same time.

Despite this, *Frankenstein Must Be Destroyed* contains some notable refinements on Hammer's Frankenstein format. For one thing, Frankenstein himself is at his most monstrous (as the title of the film might suggest). Darker-haired and apparently younger and more rigorous than he was in *Frankenstein Created Woman*, the film's opening depicts his decapitation of a fellow doctor. This is shot by Fisher so that we do not see the Baron's face (nor are we actually certain at this point that it is the Baron doing this). In the next sequence, a burglar who has broken into a laboratory is suddenly confronted by this mysterious, scythe-wielding figure who is revealed to have a horribly scarred face. A violent struggle ensues before the burglar escapes. The scarred man moves towards the camera and removes what turns out to be a mask, and we see the Baron for the first time. It is an impressive opening for the film, one which clearly sets a tone quite different from that of the gentler *Frankenstein Created Woman*. The decapitation, the image of the severed head being kicked across the laboratory floor, the level of the violence in the struggle between Frankenstein and the burglar, and, not least, the Baron himself taking on the disguise of a monster – all of them speak of an enhanced ruthlessness and an increased physicality to the proceedings (as opposed to the more ethereal concern with souls evident in *Frankenstein Created Woman*).[29]

This sense of Frankenstein himself being a more dangerous figure than before is carried over into the remainder of the film, with the Baron blackmailing a young couple into helping him transplant into another body the brain of a scientist – Brandt – who has gone mad before passing on some information that the Baron requires for his own work. As if to counteract Frankenstein's baleful influence in the film, society itself is presented as more compassionate than it was in *The Revenge of Frankenstein* (and, for the matter, in *Frankenstein Created Woman*). 'Madness is always sad', muses one of the mental health specialists dealing with Brandt, and this empathy is more than apparent in the various scenes depicting Mrs Brandt's anguish over her husband's illness. Frankenstein might be able to cure Brandt (unlike the doctors) but more strongly than ever before in Hammer's Frankenstein series it is made clear that the inhumanity this involves should be resisted. To a certain extent this involves if not a complete abandonment of then at least a diminution in the ambiguity that in earlier Fisher Frankenstein films had been associated with the Baron. He might still be part Promethean rebel, part anti-social villain in *Frankenstein Must Be Destroyed*, but his 'positive' features are only rarely evident – notably in the sequence where he confronts the other male guests at his boarding house. 'I'm afraid that stupidity always brings out the worst in me', he remarks after berating them for their ignorance and prejudice. Elsewhere in the film, however, he is a much nastier figure, especially in his dealings with Anna, the female of the couple blackmailed by him.

In *The Curse of Frankenstein*, the Baron has an affair with Justine, a castle servant (and then arranges for her to be killed), but in both *The Revenge of Frankenstein* and *Frankenstein Created Woman* he shows no sexual interest – or any other form of interest, for that matter – in women. By contrast, the relationship between the Baron and Anna is probably the most distinctive feature of *Frankenstein Must Be Destroyed* to the extent that the film can be seen as being as much about Anna's gradual subjection as it is about brain transplants. This subjection commences with Frankenstein's invading and taking control of a space initially designated as belonging to Anna – her boarding house. He makes her evict her other guests and is shown standing masterfully at the head of the stairs as she obeys his commands. Later, when Anna's fiancé begs Frankenstein to let Anna go because she is not necessary to his plans, the Baron replies that he needs her to make coffee. Later still – about half-way through the film – he rapes Anna, and at the end of the film, on discovering that she has interfered with his experiment, he stabs her to death. Anna's death is particularly unexpected for Hammer horror where the normative heterosexual couple usually survive and in this context it can be seen as a further example from Fisher's later work of an erosion of the old certainties.

Anna's rape is also, of course, a significant event, not just within *Frankenstein Must Be Destroyed* but for Fisher's work generally. It is the third and final rape to be featured in his films (that is, if one does not include the stakings of Lucy in *Dracula* and Helen in *Dracula – Prince of Darkness* as symbolic rapes). The first two – the beggar's raping the gaoler's daughter in *The Curse of the Werewolf* and Hyde's rape of Mrs Jekyll in *The Two Faces of Dr Jekyll* – are shown to derive from a male bestiality erupting to the surface. Frankenstein's rape of Anna is quite different. It is a cold, calculating act of male domination, developing from the Baron's earlier treatment of Anna and a further step towards his murdering her. Given that it fits well into this pattern of escalating victimisation, it is all the more surprising that the rape was not in the original screenplay at all but was added near the end of shooting at the insistence of Hammer boss James Carreras who felt the film needed more sex. Unsurprisingly, none of the people involved in the actual production of *Frankenstein Must Be Destroyed* were happy about this development, and the scene itself has a certain casual quality to it so far as its staging and its minimal dialogue are concerned.[30] The visual choreography of the assaults in *The Curse of the Werewolf* and *The Two Faces of Dr Jekyll* is lacking, and the scene seems to reflect the discomfort and embarrassment of the film-makers. Frankenstein just happens to be walking past a room when he sees it contains Anna alone, and without much preamble he attacks her.

The rape scene is perhaps a rare example of a crass commercial decision helping to clarify a film's identity. The authority of Frankenstein is presented not only as monstrous per se but also as founded on a ruthless and violent objectification of the woman. Throughout Fisher's 1960s horror films, a rudimentary sexual politics of male authority is gradually becoming visible, with male authority figures viewed with increasing suspicion and doubt, especially in their dealings with women. *Frankenstein Must Be Destroyed* marks the emphatic endpoint of this process; Frankenstein is utterly monstrous, Anna is utterly victimised. As before with Fisher, this is a story told from a male perspective. Anna in herself is not a particularly interesting character; it is what happens to her and what this reveals about maleness that is important for the film. And yet the critique of certain aspects of masculinity offered by the film is a telling one.

At the end of *Frankenstein Must Be Destroyed*, Frankenstein's 'creature' carries the Baron into a burning house where presumably they will both die. Compare this with the conclusion of *The Curse of Frankenstein*, released only twelve years earlier. There the Baron's walk to the scaffold is located within a rather stark moralistic framework – he has broken God's law and he must die – albeit a framework viewed with a degree of ambivalence. In contrast, the conclusion of *Frankenstein Must Be Destroyed* does not invoke any abstract morality; instead, and with a urgency absent from earlier Frankenstein films, it allies itself totally with the humanity and empathy embodied in the 'creature' and against which Frankenstein himself stands opposed.

As if in acknowledgement of the climax to the Frankenstein series provided by *Frankenstein Must Be Destroyed*, Hammer's next Frankenstein film, *The Horror of Frankenstein* (1970), was in effect a remake of *The Curse of Frankenstein* rather than a continuation of the Frankenstein story. Directed by erstwhile writer Jimmy Sangster and starring Ralph Bates as the Baron, this not very interesting film was one of several generally unsuccessful attempts by Hammer in the early 1970s to rejuvenate itself by connecting with a shifting youth market. By the time that *Frankenstein and the Monster from Hell* – the last of the Hammer Frankensteins as well as Terence Fisher's final film – was released in 1974, the Hammer horror cycle was more or less over. *The Satanic Rites of Dracula* (1973), produced after *Frankenstein and the Monster from Hell* but released a few months before, had just concluded Hammer's Dracula series, and only one more gothic horror would emerge from Hammer, the Hong Kong-produced *The Legend of the Seven Golden Vampires* (1974; Dracula – not played by Christopher Lee – makes a fleeting appearance).[31] Given that Fisher's first horror film was about Frankenstein, it seems appropriate that his final horror film should also deal with the Baron.

Even David Pirie, one of Fisher's staunchest champions, acknowledged at the time of *Frankenstein and the Monster from Hell*'s release that the film 'seems some way below the level of his best work'.[32] Yet again, the film's narrative revisits *The Revenge of Frankenstein*: the Baron has a youthful acolyte-follower, there is a passive young woman (mute through most of the film), and the creature – although more animalistic in appearance than before – possesses a humanity noticeably lacking in the Baron. However, while Frankenstein maintains his authority, he has also become a subdued, quiet figure who spends most of his time in the restricted setting of a lunatic asylum. There is a definite sense here of the shutters coming down, a sense that the Baron's experiments – once so shocking and hubristic – have by now become rather trivial and meaningless. This is particularly evident in the film's conclusion which shows the Baron, his experiment yet again a failure, sweeping up the mess and talking about starting again. The camera pulls back to reveal him as a sad, rather pathetic figure, out of place and out of time.

Frankenstein and the Monster from Hell does not really add much to the Fisher oeuvre other than this scene depicting what is essentially the Baron's redundancy. Stylistically it is competent but lacks any of the distinctive Fisher touches one finds elsewhere in his work. However, as Terence Fisher's final film, it does afford him something that so many film directors' careers have lacked – a quietly dignified exit.

Notes

1 Harry Ringel, 'Terence Fisher: the human side', *Cinefantastique*, 4:3 (1975), p. 10.
2 For more on this, see Peter Hutchings, '"We're the Martians now": British SF invasion fantasies of the 1950s and 1960s', in I. Q. Hunter (ed.), *British Science Fiction Cinema* (London, Routledge), 1999, pp. 33–47.
3 Fisher's conclusion to *The Earth Dies Screaming* bears comparison in this respect with the conclusion of Romero's *Dawn of the Dead* (1979), the first of his sequels to *The Night of the Living Dead*.
4 The film is comparable in this respect to Val Guest's 1961 film *The Day the Earth Caught Fire*. In Guest's film, the rising heat is global and has been caused by nuclear tests. Interestingly, in John Lymington's original 1959 novel of *Night of the Big Heat*, the heatwave too is global and there is some speculation that it might be the result of nuclear tests. These elements have been dropped from Fisher's 1967 adapation of the novel, presumably on the basis that so far as cinema was concerned *The Day the Earth Caught Fire* had covered this material already.
5 In Lymington's novel Jeff has not committed adultery. The stress in the film on the fallibility of the male might well not have been introduced by Fisher, but it certainly fits well into the themes he is pursuing elsewhere in the post-1962 period.
6 For a discussion of Pete Walker's work, see Steve Chibnall, *Making Mischief: The Cult Films of Pete Walker* (Guildford, Fab Press), 1998.
7 Nina Auerbach, *Our Vampires, Ourselves* (Chicago, University of Chicago Press), 1995, p. 125.
8 *Ibid.*, p. 126.
9 The puncture wounds clearly visible on the foreheads of the Gorgon's victims imply that her snake tresses have made physical contact. However, in all the attacks the Gorgon is never shown as coming that close to her victims. The puncture marks remain something of a mystery, perhaps representing an idea that was not completed due to the admittedly poor special-effect realisation of the Gorgon herself.
10 By contrast, the comparably themed Italian horror film *La Maschera del Demonio* (aka *Black Sunday* aka *The Mask of Satan*, 1960) makes great play with the similarities between the good and the evil woman, primarily by having the same actress (Barbara Steele) play both.

11 See Marcus Hearn and Alan Barnes, *The Hammer Story* (London, Titan), 1997, p. 82, for a brief discussion of this.

12 One is reminded here of a similar pairing of couples in Fisher's earlier *Four Sided Triangle* where various undesirable qualities are projected on to the couple to be destroyed, with this helping to preserve the 'purity' of the other couple (although, as I suggested in Chapter 2, this process can also undermine normality by inadvertently casting a critical light upon it).

13 David Pirie, *The Vampire Cinema* (London, Galley Press), 1977, p. 86.

14 Bram Stoker adopts much the same procedure in the original novel of *Dracula*.

15 In the 1970s Hammer would explore – perhaps exploit would be a more accurate term – the theme of the lesbian vampire in three films – *The Vampire Lovers* (1970), *Lust for a Vampire* (1970) and *Twins of Evil* (1971) – that drew upon J. Sheridan LeFanu's classic vampire story *Carmilla*. Terence Fisher was originally slated to direct *Lust for a Vampire* but illness prevented him from taking up the project.

16 Auerbach, *Our Vampires, Ourselves*, p. 128.

17 S. S. Prawer, *Caligari's Children: The Film as Tale of Terror* (Oxford, Oxford University Press), 1980, p. 257.

18 Auerbach, *Our Vampires, Ourselves*, p. 129.

19 *Ibid.*, p. 128.

20 David Pirie, *A Heritage of Horror: The English Gothic Cinema 1946–1972* (London, Gordon Fraser), 1973, p. 156.

21 *Ibid.*, p. 77.

22 This 'straightness' is perfectly congruent with Fisher's other work, but before we start viewing him as the sole 'straight man' of British horror, it's worth noting that Michael Reeves' *The Sorcerers* features an old woman gaining mental control of a young man's body. As with *Frankenstein Created Woman*, the same-sex implications of this are largely avoided through stressing the possession theme.

23 Pirie, *A Heritage of Horror*, p. 77.

24 *Ibid.*, pp. 61–3.

25 The history of Hammer is littered with many unrealised projects, but of all of these *I Am Legend* is the most tantalising, one of the great might-have-beens of British horror. *I Am Legend* was subsequently filmed in 1964 as *The Last Man on Earth* (directed by Sidney Salkow and starring Vincent Price, with a screenplay written in part by Matheson under the name 'Logan Swanson') and in 1971 as *The Omega Man* (directed by Boris Sagal and starring Charlton Heston). Neither of these proved particularly satisfactory adaptations of Matheson's original (although *The Omega Man* is an interesting film in its own right). A new version – to be directed by British film-maker Ridley Scott and starring Arnold Schwarzenegger – was briefly mooted in the late 1990s but the proposed project came to nothing.

26 For a discussion of Matheson's literary work, see Mark Jancovich, *Rational Fears: American Horror in the 1950s* (Manchester, Manchester University Press), 1996, pp. 129–65.

27 Quoted in Dennis Wheatley, *The Time Has Come ... : Drink and Ink, 1919–1977* (London, Hutchinson), 1979, p. 260.

28 This transition from assistant director to screenwriter was not unprece- dented for Hammer. Jimmy Sangster, Hammer's principal horror writer in the early years of horror production, had followed a similar route. However, Bert Batt was not to receive any further screenwriting credits.

29 So effective and memorable an introduction is the opening of *Frankenstein Must Be Destroyed* that I recall it being used to introduce a personal appear- ance by Peter Cushing himself on stage at the National Film Theatre in March 1986.

30 See David Miller, *The Peter Cushing Companion* (London, Reynolds & Hearn), 2000, p. 122, for a brief discussion of the filming of the scene.

31 Hammer would produce one more horror film – an adaptation, with contemporary settings, of Dennis Wheatley's *To the Devil a Daughter* (1976).

32 *Monthly Film Bulletin*, 41:483 (April 1974), p. 72.

Conclusion

Auteurist accounts of the role of the director in cinema have often invoked a certain heroism, the heroism of the auteur-director as he attempts to transcend industrial constraints in order to produce work of lasting value, and, more implicitly, the critic's heroism in saving the auteur's films from critical oblivion. This has not been the view of the director offered by this book. Instead of seeing Terence Fisher as someone who stood opposed to a philistine industry, I have sought to show Fisher as a director dependent on and at ease with the industrial and collaborative nature of film-making. In a fundamental sense, what value there is in Terence Fisher's work (and I believe there is considerable value) exists because of the British film industry and the opportunities it afforded Fisher, not despite the industry. It follows that an evaluation of Fisher's career also involves an evaluation of the sectors of the industry through which that career passed.

Elsewhere I have argued that looking at the director has served two distinct functions in recent writings on British cinema. The first is the traditional evaluative one – i.e. British cinema is worth-while because it contains directors of distinction. The second, which often coexists with the first, uses the study of directors as one way of exploring particular areas of British cinema.[1] Both of these functions are readily apparent, for instance, in David Pirie's *A Heritage of Horror: The English Gothic Cinema 1946–1972* which intertwines an evaluation of Fisher as auteur (along with some other director studies) with a more general account of British horror cinema. Fisher himself emerges from this as a film-maker who produced work that was distinctive while also typifying a certain area of British film.

This double focus has informed my own account of Fisher. Studying his career has helped bring into view parts of British cinema that up until recently have remained in relative (and undeserved) obscurity – notably Highbury, post-war Gainsborough (other than the well-known costume melodramas) and the British 1950s B movie. The fact that Fisher's career encompassed these elements along with Hammer horror is also quite revealing inasmuch as it highlights the sort of connections that exist between different parts of the industry, and how these connections might be transformed over time. Seen in this way, Fisher's progression from post-war Gainsborough via B movies to Hammer's exploitation cinema becomes an expression of broader changes in the industry, and particularly its increasing reliance on American markets and American finance.

At the same time, I have sought to preserve and even develop the idea of Fisher as a director whose films are in various ways significant and valuable because of Fisher's input into them. I have not just considered the horror work in this respect – although these horrors are a key feature of Fisher's oeuvre – but have looked at his directorial career as a whole. In part, this has involved thinking about the films as artefacts, with Fisher's input less to do with his 'authorial vision' and more with his application of certain film-making skills, notably his considerable compositional and staging abilities. However, I have also identified a set of thematic concerns apparent in Fisher's work, intermittently expressed in the first part of the career, expressed rather more forcefully in that career's latter stages.

Of course, identifying a director's films as distinctive does not necessarily translate into their being good films. The question of value is a difficult one, especially in respect of a director like Terence Fisher about whom there is not really a critical consensus. Throughout his career, Fisher received very little critical attention. From the 1970s onwards his reputation has fluctuated. Praised by David Pirie in the early 1970s as a Gothic auteur, he has since come to be seen by some as the reactionary face of British horror against which more radical and innovative approaches can be defined. This book has presented Fisher as a more complex figure than this, as not entirely the auteur identified by Pirie but neither the wholly reactionary film-maker imagined by others. A survey of the whole career reveals him instead as someone whose films traded as much in anxiety as they did in authority, and, so far as his horror work is concerned, as a director as much caught up in a process of generic change as some of the younger British and American horror directors who would come to the fore from the late 1960s onwards. Isabel Cristina Pinedo has suggested that Hammer horror forms a transitional stage between 'classical horror' (1930s US horror) and more modern forms of horror, and Fisher's horror films perhaps represent more clearly than other Hammer horrors some of the tensions and uncertainties involved in this transition.[2] One can further argue that it is primarily in this sense of Fisher's work in general (and not just his horror work) – in its conjoining of certainty and doubt, authority and subjection, cruelty and compassion – that not only his distinctiveness but also his value as a film-maker resides.

My own fascination with the films of Terence Fisher has endured for twenty-five years and I suspect it will continue. Inevitably there have been periods when I stopped seeing the films, but the films – or, to be more precise, moments from the films – have always been with me. I think here of Christopher Lee's first appearances in *The Curse of Frankenstein* and *Dracula*, and also from *Dracula* Van Helsing's graveyard confrontation with Lucy and his final battle with the Count, of Kharis's attack on John Banning in *The Mummy*, of the openings of *The Hound of the Baskervilles* and *The Curse of the Werewolf*, of Dirk Bogarde throwing a chair through a wall in *So Long at the Fair*, of Alan's death and Dracula's resurrection in *Dracula – Prince of Darkness*, of the conclusion of *Frankenstein Created Woman*. Most of all, perhaps, I think of that moment from near the end of *The Devil Rides Out* when De Richleau opens the library door and sees Tanith and Rex walking towards him through the early morning mist (surely one of the most beautiful images ever to grace a British film).

'What films are showing at a cinema inside you?' novelist Jeanette Winterson once asked.[3] It's a question to which all those who care about cinema should attend. Of course, there will be as many answers as there are people answering, but there will always be overlaps, shared connections with particular films. I am aware from my own experience that my own feelings about Fisher's work are shared by others, that these feelings are something more than a private cinephile fancy (although they are also that). This suggests that Fisher's films do not just exist in relation to a certain social and industrial history, the 'official' or public history, but also maintain a presence within memory, the memories of individuals as well as a more collective, shared memory. Needless to say, this is a very speculative way of thinking about the director. It is hard to prove it by reference to empirical evidence; it can only really be apprehended through one's own personal experience of cinema (which can then be communicated to others in the hope that someone out there understands). Yet it seems to me that this way of thinking is, or should be, an important dimension of any appreciation of Fisher's work (or, for that matter, the work of any other director). If these films matter, it is because people care about them enough to remember them. All the articles and books I have read that offer positive accounts of Fisher share with my own book a passion for his work, a passion that so far as I am aware has not been generated by directors working in similar positions to Fisher in the British film industry.

What Terence Fisher himself would have made of this is another matter entirely. One suspects a certain bemusement (or amusement) and embarrassment would have ensued. Fisher once described himself as 'a working director', and throughout his career he steadfastly defined his activities in relation to the industry's standards of professionalism. Such a career trajectory seems a million miles away from the language that is sometimes used – not least in this book – to describe his films, the language of desire and passion. Interestingly, however, the films themselves often set up and rely upon a tension between a materialistic, quotidian reality and dangerous but fascinating worlds of desire. Perhaps the most remarkable aspect of Fisher's work in this respect was that a director working in the lower reaches of British cinema with minimal resources was able to conjure up such fantastic worlds and do this with such power and conviction. For this reason alone, the films of Terence Fisher are worth remembering.

Notes

1 Peter Hutchings, 'The histogram and the list: the director in British film criticism', *The Journal of Popular British Cinema*, 4 (2001).
2 Isabel Cristina Pinedo, *Recreational Terror: Women and the Pleasures of Horror Film Viewing* (New York, State University of New York Press), 1997, p. 138.
3 Jeanette Winterson, 'Blooded with optimism', *Sight and Sound*, 1:1 (May 1991), p. 33.

Filmography

Most of the information included in this filmography comes either from the films themselves or from publicity material issued by production companies. Supplementary sources of information include journals *Film Dope* and *The Monthly Film Bulletin* as well as Denis Gifford's invaluable *The British Film Catalogue 1895–1970: A Guide to Entertainment Films* (Newton Abbot, David & Charles, 1973) and Dave Rogers' *The ITV Encyclopedia of Adventure* (London, Boxtree, 1988).

Editorial credits

Terence Fisher worked as an editor from 1936 onwards, first at Gainsborough and subsequently at Warner Brothers–First National with some work done elsewhere for less well-known companies such as Greenspan & Seligman and British Aviation. What follows is an indicative rather than a definitive listing of his credits. Given that so many films and associated records from this period are apparently lost, it seems unlikely that an authoritatively complete list of Fisher's work as an editor will ever be possible.

For Gainsborough: *Jack of All Trades* (1936, d. Jack Hulbert/Robert Stevenson), *Tudor Rose* (1936, d. Robert Stevenson), *Where There's a Will* (1936, d. William Beaudine), *Everybody Dance* (1936, d. Charles Reisner), *Windbag the Sailor* (1936, d. William Beaudine) – and, after some years away from the studio, *The Wicked Lady* (1945, d. Leslie Arliss).

For Warner Brothers–First National: *Mr Satan* (1938, d. Arthur Woods), *George and Margaret* (1940, d. George King), *Atlantic Ferry*

(1941, d. Walter Forde), *Flying Fortress* (1942, d. Walter Forde), *The Peterville Diamond* (1942, d. Walter Forde), *The Night Invader* (1942, d. Herbert Mason), *The Dark Tower* (1943, d. John Harlow), *The Hundred Pound Window* (1943, d. Brian Desmond Hurst), *Flight from Folly* (1944, d. Herbert Mason).

Other credits included *On the Night of the Fire* (1939, d. Brian Desmond Hurst) for Greenspan & Seligman, *The 7th Survivor* (1941, d. Leslie Hiscott) for British National–Shaftesbury, *Tomorrow We Live* (1942, d. George King) and *Candlelight in Algeria* (1943, d. George King) for British Aviation, *One Exciting Night* (1944, d. Walter Forde) for Columbia British, and, as Fisher's final editorial credit, *The Master of Bankdam* (1947, d. Walter Forde) for Holbein.

Television credits

As with his editing credits, a definitive listing of Fisher's television work is probably not possible, and while researching this book I was unable to track down any of his TV work for viewing. The series upon which he worked included *Douglas Fairbanks Presents* (1953–1957), *Colonel March Of Scotland Yard* (1956–1957), *The Adventures of Robin Hood* (1956–1960) – the episodes (all from Seasons 1 and 2) 'Trial by Battle', 'The Traitor', 'The Thorkill Ghost', 'Ransom', 'The Hero', 'Hubert', 'The Dream', 'The Blackbird', 'The Path of True Love' and 'The Infidel' – *Assignment Foreign Legion* (1957), *The Gay Cavalier* (1957) – the episodes 'Springtime for Julia', 'The Sealed Knot' and 'Girl of Quality' – *Dial 999* (1958–1959) and *Sword of Freedom* (1959–1961). Of these, *Colonel March Of Scotland Yard* sounds the most intriguing. Based on stories by John Dickson Carr and starring Boris Karloff as the eponymous Colonel, its narratives seem to have contained pronounced supernatural elements.

Directorial credits

Film dates refer to the film's initial British release rather than the date of its production.

I have decided not to include in the filmography *The Gelignite Gang* (aka *The Dynamiters*, 1956) although it is sometimes attributed to Fisher, notably by Denis Gifford in *The British Film Catalogue 1895–*

1970. Other sources attribute it as a co-directed project to Fisher and Francis Searle. In *The Charm of Evil: The Life and Films of Terence Fisher* (Metuchen, NJ and London, Scarecrow Press), 1991, p. 218, Wheeler Winston Dixon speculates that Fisher might have done some work on the film, although he does this on the basis of seeing a version of the film lacking a directorial credit. The version I have seen does have a directorial credit; it reads 'Directed by Francis Searle'. In a recent interview – in Brian McFarlane's *An Autobiography of British Cinema* (London, Methuen), 1997, pp. 522–6 – Searle himself has reminisced briefly about the film's production and given no indication that the film was co-directed. In the absence of hard evidence to the contrary, one has to suppose that in this case the usually ultra-reliable Gifford made a mistake (his entry on the film does not even mention Searle).

However, I have included *Three's Company* – which contains material shot by Fisher for the television series *Douglas Fairbanks Presents* – because it did achieve a British theatrical release.

Colonel Bogey 1947, 51 min.

Production company/studio: Highbury
Producer: John Croydon
Screenplay: John Baines, W. E. C. Fairchild
Photography: Gordon Lang
Editor: Gordon Pilkington
Art director: Don Russell
Music: Norman Fulton
Cast: Mary Jerrold (Aunt Mabel), Jane Barrett (Alice Graham), Jack Train (Uncle James), John Stone (Wilfred Barriteau), Hedli Anderson (Millicent), Ethel Coleridge (Emily)

To The Public Danger 1948, 44 min.

Production company/studio: Highbury
Producer: John Croydon
Screenplay: T. J. Morrison and Arthur Reid from Patrick Hamilton's radio play
Photography: Harry Waxman, Roy Fogwell
Editor: Graeme Hamilton
Production designer: Ken Sharp

Music: Doreen Carwithen
Cast: Dermot Walsh (Captain Cole), Susan Shaw (Nancy Bedford),
Roy Plomley (Reggie), Barry Letts (Fred Lane), Betty Ann Davies
(Barmaid), Patricia Hayes (Postmistress), Sam Kydd (Police
Driver), John Lorrell (Police Sergeant), Frederick Piper (Labourer),
Patience Rentoul (Labourer's wife)

Song For Tomorrow 1948, 62 min.

Production company/studio: Highbury
Producer: Ralph Nunn-May
Screenplay: W. E. C. Fairchild
Photography: Walter J. Harvey
Editor: Gordon Pilkington
Art director: Donald Russell
Music: William Blezard
Cast: Evelyn McCabe (Helen Maxwell), Ralph Michael (Roger Stanton),
Shaun Noble (Derek Wardell), James Hayter (Nicholas Klausmann),
Valentine Dunn (Mrs Wardell), Christopher Lee (Auguste), Ethel
Coleridge (Woman in cinema), Yvonne Foster (Nurse), Carleen
Lord (Helen's dresser), Conrad Phillips (Lieutenant Fenton), Martin
Boddey (Major), Sam Kydd (Sergeant), Lockwood West (Mr
Stokes)

Portrait From Life 1948, 90 min.

Production company: Gainsborough
Studio: Shepherd's Bush
Producer: Antony Darnborough
Screenplay: Frank Harvey Jnr., Muriel Box and Sydney Box, from an
original story by David Evans
Photography: Jack Asher
Editor: V. Sagovsky
Supervising art director: George Provis
Music: Benjamin Frankel
Cast: Guy Rolfe (Lawrence), Mai Zetterling (Hildegard/Lydia), Robert
Beatty (Campbell Reid), Herbert Lom (Hendlmann), Arnold Marlé
(Menzel) and in order of appearance Peter Murray (Lieut. Keith),
Thora Hird (Mrs Skinner), Eric Messiter (Coroner), Cyril Chamber-
lain (Supervisor), Patrick Holt (Ferguson), Betty Lynne (Woman

Interpreter), Dorothea Glade (Hildegarde Schmidt), Nellie Arno (Anna Skutetsky), Richard Molinas (Man in crowd), Hugo Schuster (Interpreter), Gordon Bell (Capt. Roberts), Sam Kydd (Army Truck Driver), Gerard Heinz (Heine), Sybilla Binder (Eitel), George Thorpe (Brigadier), Philo Hauser (Hans), Eric Pohlmann (Leader of search party)

Marry Me! 1949, 97 min.

Production company: Gainsborough
Producer: Betty Box
Screenplay: Denis Waldock, Lewis Gilbert
Photography: Ray Elton
Editor: Gordon Pilkington
Art director: George Provis
Music: Clifton Parker
Cast: Derek Bond (Andrew Scott), Susan Shaw (Pat Cooper), Patrick Holt (Martin Roberts), Carol Marsh (Doris Pearson), David Tomlinson (David Haig), Zena Marshall (Marcelle), Guy Middleton (Sir George Blake), Nora Swinburne (Enid Lawson), Brenda Bruce (Brenda Delamere), Jean Cadell (Hester Parsons), Mary Jerrold (Emily Parsons), Denis O'Dea (Saunders), Yvonne Owen (Sue Carson), Alison Leggatt (Miss Beamish), Beatrice Varley (Mrs Perrins), Cyril Chamberlain (PC Jackson), Hal Osmond (Man in restaurant), Russell Waters (Mr Pearson), Joan Hickson (Mrs Pearson), Marianne Stone (Elsie), J. H. Roberts (Old Gent in Train), Lyn Evans (Railway Official), Anthony Steel (Jack Harris)

The Astonished Heart 1949, 89 min.

(co-directed with Antony Darnborough)
Production company: Gainsborough
Studio: Pinewood
Producer: Antony Darnborough
Screenplay: Noel Coward from his own play
Photography: Jack Asher
Editor: V. Sagovsky
Supervising art director: George Provis
Music: Noel Coward
Cast: Noel Coward (Christian Faber), Celia Johnson (Barbara Faber),

Margaret Leighton (Leonora Vail), Joyce Carey (Susan Birch), Graham Payn (Tim Verney), Amy Veness (Alice Smith), Ralph Michael (Philip Lucas), Michael Hordern (Ernest), Patricia Glyn (Helen), Alan Webb (Sir Reginald), Everly Gregg (Miss Harper), John Salew (Soames), Gerald Anderson (Waiter), John Warren (Barman)

So Long at the Fair 1950, 86 min.

(co-directed with Antony Darnborough)
Production company: Gainsborough
Studio: Pinewood
Producer: Betty E. Box
Screenplay: Hugh Mills, Anthony Thorne
Photography: Reginald Wyer
Editor: Gordon Hales
Supervising art director: George Provis
Music: Benjamin Frankel
Cast: Jean Simmons (Vicky Barton), Dirk Bogarde (George Hathaway), David Tomlinson (Johnny Barton), Honor Blackman (Rhoda O'Donovan), Cathleen Nesbitt (Madame Herve), Felix Aylmer (Consul), Betty Warren (Mrs O'Donovan), Marcel Poncin (Narcisse), Austin Trevor (Commissaire), Andre Morell (Dr Hart), Zena Marshall (Nina), Eugene Deckers (Day Porter)

Home to Danger 1951, 66 min.

Production company: New World/Lance Comfort Productions
Producer: Lance Comfort
Screenplay: Francis Edge, John Temple-Smith
Photography: Reg Wyer
Editor: Francis Edge
Art director: Cedric Dawe
Music: M. Arnold
Cast: Rona Anderson (Barbara), Guy Rolfe (Robert), Francis Lister (Wainwright), Alan Wheatley (Hughes), Stanley Baker (Willie Dougan), Denis Harkin (Jimmy-the-one), Bruce Belfrage (Solicitor)

The Last Page 1952, 84 min.

Production company: Exclusive-Lippert (Hammer)
Studio: Bray
Producer: Anthony Hinds
Screenplay: Frederick Knott from a play by James Hadley Chase
Photography: Walter Harvey
Editor: Maurice Rootes
Cast: George Brent (Harman), Marguerite Chapman (Stella), Raymond Huntley (Clive), Peter Reynolds (Jeff), Diana Dors (Ruby), Eleanor Summerfield (Vi), Meredith Edwards (Dale), Isobel Dean (May Harman), Harry Fowler (Joe), Nelly Arno (Miss Rosetti), Conrad Phillips (Todd), Lawrence Ward (Lang), David Keir (Mr Quince), Eleanore Bryan (Mary), Jack Faint (Receptionist), Harold Goodwin (Waiter), Leslie Weston (Mr Bruce), Courtney Hope (Woman Customer), John Mann (The Tobacconist), Archie Duncan (PC Gibbons), Lawrence O'Madden (Elderly Customer), Ian Wilson (Second Customer)

Wings of Danger 1952, 73 min.

Production company: Hammer
Studio: Riverside
Producer: Anthony Hinds
Screenplay: John Gilling from the novel *Dead on Course* by Elleston Trevor and Packham Webb
Photography: Walter Harvey
Editor: Jim Needs
Art director: Andrew Mazzei
Musical director: Malcolm Arnold
Cast: Zachary Scott (Vaness), Robert Beatty (Nick), Naomi Chance (Avril), Arthur Lane (Boyd), Kay Kendall (Alexia), Colin Tapley (Maxwell), Harold Lang (Snell), Diana Cilento (Jeannette), Jack Allen (Truscott), Ian Fleming (Talbot), Douglas Muir (Doctor), Sheila Raynor (Nurse), Courtney Hope (Mrs C. Smith), Nigel Neilson (Duty Officer), Darcy Conyers (Signal Operator), Kathleen Stuart (Receptionist), Anthony Miles (Sam), Laurie Taylor (O'Gorman), June Ashley, June Mitchell and Natasha Sokolova (Three Blondes)

Stolen Face 1952, 72 min.

Production Company: Exclusive (Hammer)
Studio: Riverside
Producer: Anthony Hinds
Screenplay: Martin Berkley and Richard Landau, based on an original
    story by Alexander Paal and Steven Vas
Photography: Walter Harvey
Editor: Maurice Rootes
Music: Malcolm Arnold
Cast: Lizabeth Scott (Alice Brent and Lily B), Paul Henreid (Dr Philip
    Ritter), Andre Morell (David), John Wood (Jack), Mary Mackenzie
    (Lily A), Arnold Ridley (Russell), Susan Stephen (Betty), Cyril
    Smith (Alf), Diana Beaumont (May), Terence O'Regan (Pete),
    Russell Napier (Cutler), Ambrosine Phillpots (Miss Patton), Everly
    Gregg (Lady Harringay), Alexis France (Mrs Emmett), John Bull
    (Charles Emmett), Richard Wattis (Wentworth), Dorothy Bramhall
    (Miss Simpson), Janet Burnell (Maggie), Grace Gavin (Nurse),
    William Murray (Floor Walker), John Warren (Railway Guard),
    Anna Turner (Maid), Hal Osmond (Photographer), Philip Vickers
    (Soldier), James Valentine (Sailor), Howard Douglas (1st farmer),
    Brookes Turner (2nd farmer)

Distant Trumpet 1952, 63 min.

Production company: Meridian
Producer: Derek Elphinstone
Screenplay: Derek Elphinstone
Photography: Gordon Lang
Editor: John Seabourne
Art director: George Jones
Music: David Jenkins
Cast: Derek Bond (David Anthony), Jean Patterson (Valerie Maitland),
    Derek Elphinstone (Richard Anthony), Grace Gavin (Miss Philips
    – 'Flips'), Anne Brooke (Beryl Jeffreys), Jean Webster-Brough (Mrs
    Waterhouse)

Four Sided Triangle 1953, 81 min.

Production company: Hammer
Studio: Bray
Producer: Michael Carreras and Alexander Paal
Screenplay: Paul Tabori and Terence Fisher from William F. Temple's
    novel
Photography: Reginald Wyer
Editor: Maurice Rootes
Art director: J. Elder Wills
Music: Malcolm Arnold
Cast: Barbara Payton (Lena and Helen), Stephen Murray (Bill), James
    Hayter (Dr Harvey), John Van Eyssen (Robin), Percy Marmont (Sir
    Walter), Kynaston Reeves (Lord Grant), Jennifer Dearman (Lena
    as a child), Glyn Dearman (Bill as a child), Sean Barrett (Robin as a
    child), John Stuart (Solicitor), Edith Saville (Lady Grant)

Mantrap 1953, 78 min.

Production company: Hammer
Studio: Bray
Producer: Michael Carreras and Alexander Paal
Screenplay: Paul Tabori and Terence Fisher, adapted by Tabori from
    Elleston Trevor's *Queen in Danger*
Photography: Reginald Wyer
Editor: Jim Needs
Art director: J. Elder Wills (credited simply as Elder Wills)
Music: Doreen Carwithen
Cast: Paul Henreid (Bishop), Lois Maxwell (Thelma), Kieron Moore
    (Speight), Hugh Sinclair (Jerrard), Kay Kendall (Vera), Lloyd Lamble
    (Frisnay), Anthony Forwood (Rex), Bill Travers (Victor), Mary
    Laura Wood (Susie), Liam Gaffney (Dorval), John Penrose (Du
    Vancet), Conrad Phillips (Barker), John Stuart (Doctor), Anna
    Turner (Marjorie), Christina Forrest (Joanna), Arnold Diamond
    (Alphonse), Jane Welsh (Laura), Geoffrey Murphy (Plain Clothes
    Man), Terry Carney (Detective), Sally Newland (Receptionist),
    Barbara Kowin (Fashion Commere)

Spaceways 1953, 76 min.

Production company: Hammer
Producer: Michael Carreras
Screenplay: Paul Tabori and Richard Landau from a radio play by
    Charles Eric Maine
Photography: Reginald Wyer
Editor: Maurice Rootes
Art director: J. Elder Wills
Music: Ivor Slaney
Cast: Howard Duff (Stephen Mitchell), Eva Bartok (Lisa Frank),
    Andrew Osborn (Philip Crenshaw), Alan Wheatley (Smith), Philip
    Leaver (Dr Keppler), Michael Medwin (Toby Andrews), Cecile
    Chevreau (Vanessa), Anthony Ireland (General Hays), David Horne
    (Cabinet Minister)

Blood Orange 1953, 76 min.

Production company: Hammer
Studio: Bray
Producer: Michael Carreras
Screenplay: Jan Read
Photography: Jimmy Harvey
Editor: Maurice Rootes
Art director: J. Elder Wills
Musical Director: Ivor Slaney
Cast: Tom Conway (Conway), Naomi Chance (Gina), Mila Parely
    (Helen Pascal), Eric Pohlman (Mercedes), Andrew Osborn (Captain
    Colin Simpson), Richard Wattis (Detective Inspector MacLeod),
    Margaret Halstan (Lady Marchant), Eileen Way (Mme Fernande),
    Michael Ripper (Eddie), Betty Cooper (Miss Betty), Thomas
    Heathcote (Detective Sergeant Jessup), Alan Rolfe (Inspector),
    Roger Delgado (Marlowe), Reed DeRoven (Heath), Delphi Lawrence
    (Chelsea), Christine Forrest (Blonde), Ann Hanslip (Jane), Davy
    Leon (George), Dorothy Robson (Seamstress), Leo Phillips (Harry),
    Robert Moore (Stevenson), Denis Cowles (Commissionaire), John
    H. Watson (Chauffeur), Cleo Rose (Vivian)

Note that some reference books list Tom Conway as playing
himself in this film. However, it is clear from the film itself that
Conway is playing a private detective who just happens to be called

Tom Conway. I have no explanation for this little piece of bizarreness. Presumably it made sense at the time.

Three's Company 1953, 78 min.

Fisher directed two segments – 'The Surgeon' and 'Take a Number' – while Charles Saunders directed 'The Scream'.
Production company: Douglas Fairbanks, Jnr
Screenplay: Richard Alan Simmons and Larry Marcus ('The Surgeon'), Larry Marcus ('Take a Number')
Photography: Jimmy Wilson, Brendan Stafford
Editor: Inman Hunt, Sam Simmonds
Art direction: Norman Arnold
Music: Allan Gray
Three's Company was a compendium of material originally shot for the *Douglas Fairbanks Presents* TV series.

Face the Music 1954, 84 min.

Production company: Hammer
Studio: Bray
Producer: Michael Carreras
Screenplay: Ernest Borneman from his novel
Photography: Jimmy Harvey
Editor: Maurice Rootes
Art director: J. Elder Wills
Musical directors: Ivor Slaney and Kenny Baker
Cast: Alex Nichol (James Bradley), Eleanor Summerfield (Barbara Quigley), John Salew (Max Margulis), Paul Carpenter (Johnny Sutherland), Geoffrey Keen (Maurice Green), Ann Hanslip (Maxine), Fred Johnson (Detective Sergeant MacKenzie), Arthur Lane (Jeff Colt), Martin Boddey (Inspector Mulrooney), Paula Byrne (Gloria Lewis Colt), Leo Phillips (Dresser), Freddie Tripp (Stage Manager), Ben Williams (Gatekeeper), Frank Birch (Trumpet Salesman), Jeremy Hawk (Recording Technician), James Carney (Mickey) and Kenny Baker's Dozen (Melvin Hayes, who would later play the young Baron in *The Curse of Frankenstein* appears briefly in an uncredited walk-on part.)

The Stranger Came Home 1954, 78 min.

Production company: Exclusive (Hammer)
Producer: Michael Carreras
Screenplay: Michael Carreras from George Sanders' novel *Stranger at Home*
Photography: Jim Harvey
Editor: Bill Lenny
Art director: J. Elder Wills
Music: Leonard Salzedo, Ivor Slaney
Cast: Paulette Goddard (Angie), William Sylvester (Philip Vickers), Patrick Holt (Job Crandall), Paul Carpenter (Bill Saul), Alvys Maben (Joan Merrill), Russell Napier (Inspector Traherne)

Mask of Dust 1954, 79 min.

Production company: Hammer
Studio: Bray
Executive producer: Michael Carreras
Producer: Mickey Delamar
Screenplay: Richard Landau from a novel by Jon Manchip White
Photography: Jimmy Harvey
Editor: Bill Lenny
Art director: J. Elder Wills
Music: Leonard Salzedo
Cast: Richard Conte (Peter Wells), Mari Aldon (Pat Wells), George Coulouris (Dallapiccola), Peter Illing (Bellario), Alec Mango (Guido Rizetti), Meredith Edwards (Lawrence), James Copeland (Johnny), Edwin Richfield, Richard Marner, Tim Turner, Jeremy Hawk and as themselves Stirling Moss, Reg Parnell, John Cooper, Alan Brown, Geoffrey Taylor, Leslie Marr

Final Appointment 1954, 69 min.

Production company: A. C. T. Films
Studio: Nettlefold
Producer: Francis Searle
Screenplay: Kenneth Hayles, adapted from the play *Death Keeps a Date* by Sidney Nelson and Maurice Harrison
Photography: Jonah Jones

Editor: John Ferris
Art director: C. P. Norman
Cast: John Bentley (Mike Billings), Eleanor Summerfield (Jenny), Hubert Gregg (Hartnell), Liam Redmond (Inspector Corcoran), Jean Lodge (Laura Robens), Meredith Edwards (Tom Martin), Sam Kydd (Vickery), Charles Farrell (Percy), Peter Bathurst (Harold Williams), Arthur Lowe (Barratt), Gerald Case (Australian Official), Jessica Cairns (War Office Typist), Tony Hilton (Jimmy), Henry De Bray (Restaurant Manager), John H. Watson (Police Sergeant)

Children Galore 1954, 60 min.

Production company: Grendon Films
Studio: Brighton
Producer: Henry Passmore
Screenplay: John and Emery Bonett and Peter Plaskitt
Photography: Jonah Jones
Editor: Inman Hunter
Art director: John Elphick
Cast: Eddie Byrne (Zacky Jones), June Thorburn (Milly Ark), Betty Ann Davies (Mrs Ark), Richard Leach (Harry Bunnion), Marjorie Rhodes (Ada Jones), Jack McNaughton (Pat Ark), Violet Gould (Mrs Bunnion), Peter Evan Thomas (Lord Redscarfe), Marjorie Hume (Lady Redscarfe), Lucy Griffiths (Miss Prescott), Henry Caine (Bert Bunnion)

Murder by Proxy 1955, 87 min.

Production company: Hammer
Producer: Michael Carreras
Screenplay: Richard Landau from a novel by Helen Nielsen
Photography: Jimmy Harvey
Editor: Maurice Rootes
Art director: Jim Elder Wills
Music: Ivor Slaney
Cast: Dane Clark (Casey Morrow), Belinda Lee (Phyllis Brunner), Eleanor Summerfield (Maggie Doone), Andrew Osborn (Lance Gordon), Betty Ann Davies (Alicia Brunner), Jill Melford (Miss Nardis), Harold Lang (Travis), Michael Golden (Inspector Johnson)

The Flaw 1955, 61 min.

Production company: Cybex
Producer: Geoffrey Goodhart and Brandon Fleming
Screenplay: Brandon Fleming
Photography: Cedric Williams
Editor: Carmen Belaieff
Cast: John Bentley (Paul Oliveri), Donald Houston (John Millway), Rona Anderson (Monica), Doris Yorke (Mrs Bower), Tonia Bern (Vera), J. Trevor Davis (Sir George Bentham), Cecilia Cavendish (Lady Bentham)

Stolen Assignment 1955, 62 min.

Production company: A. C. T. Films
Studio: Bray
Producer: Francis Searle
Screenplay: Kenneth Hayles from a story by Sidney Nelson and Maurice Harrison
Photography: James Harvey
Editor: John Pomeroy
Art director: William Kellner
Cast: John Bentley (Mike Billings), Hy Hazell (Jenny Drew), Eddie Byrne (Inspector Corcoran), Patrick Holt (Henry Crossley), Joyce Carey (Ida Garnett), Kay Callard (Stella Watson), Violet Gould (Mrs Hudson), Jessica Cairns (Marilyn Dawn), Charles Farrell (Percy Simpson), Michael Ellison (Danny Hudson), Desmond Rayner (John Smith), Graham Stuart (Coroner), Frank Forsyth (Dr Roberts), Clement Hamelin (Seth Makepeace), John H. Watson (Plain Clothes Detective Sergeant), Raymond Rollett (Desk Sergeant)

The Last Man to Hang? 1956, 75 min.

Production company: A. C. T. Films
Producer: John Gossage
Screenplay: Ivor Montagu and Max Trell, adapted by Gerald Bullett and Maurice Elvey from the novel *The Jury* by Gerald Bullett
Photography: Desmond Dickinson
Editor: Peter Taylor
Art director: Alan Harris

Music: John Wooldridge

Cast: Tom Conway (Sir Roderick Strood), Elizabeth Sellers (Daphne Strood), Eunice Gayson (Elizabeth Anders), Freda Jackson (Mrs Tucker), Hugh Latimer (Mark Perryman), Raymond Huntley (Attorney General), Margaretta Scott (Mrs Cranshaw)

Kill Me Tomorrow 1957, 80 min.

Production company: Delta Films

Studio: Southall

Producer: Francis Searle

Screenplay: Robert Falconer and Manning O'Brine, from an original story by Robert Falconer

Photography: Geoffrey Faithful

Editor: Ann Chegwidden

Art director: Bernard Robinson

Music: Temple Abady

Cast: Pat O'Brien (Bart Crosbie), Lois Maxwell (Jill Brook), George Coulouris (Heinz Webber), Robert Brown (Steve), Ronald Adam (Brook), Richard Pasco (Dr Fisher), Wensley Pithey (Inspector Lane), Freddie Mills (Waxie) plus Tommy Steele

The Curse of Frankenstein 1957, 83 min.

Production company: Hammer

Studio: Bray

Producer: Anthony Hinds

Screenplay: Jimmy Sangster

Photography: Jack Asher

Editor: James Needs

Production designer: Bernard Robinson

Music: James Bernard

Cast: Peter Cushing (Victor Frankenstein), Hazel Court (Elizabeth), Robert Urquhart (Paul Krempe), Christopher Lee (Creature), Melvyn Hayes (Young Victor), Valerie Gaunt (Justine), Paul Hardtmuth (Professor Bernstein), Noel Hood (Aunt), Fred Johnson (Grandpa), Claude Kingston (Little Boy), Alex Gallier (Priest), Michael Mulcaster (Warder), Andrew Leigh (Burgomaster), Ann Blake (Wife), Sally Walsh (Young Elizabeth), Middleton Woods (Lecturer), Raymond Ray (Uncle)

Dracula 1958, 82 min.

Production company: Hammer
Studio: Bray
Producer: Anthony Hinds
Screenplay: Jimmy Sangster
Photography: Jack Asher
Supervising editor: James Needs
Production designer: Bernard Robinson
Music: James Bernard
Cast: Peter Cushing (Dr Van Helsing), Christopher Lee (Dracula), Michael Gough (Arthur), Melissa Stribling (Mina), Carol Marsh (Lucy), Olga Dickie (Gerda), John Van Eyssen (Jonathan), Valerie Gaunt (Vampire Woman), Janine Faye (Tania), Barbara Archer (Inga), Charles Lloyd Pack (Dr Seward), George Merritt (Policeman), George Woodbridge (Landlord), George Benson (Official), Miles Malleson (Undertaker), Geoffrey Bayldon (Porter), Paul Cole (Lad)

The Revenge of Frankenstein 1958, 89 min.

Production company: Hammer
Studio: Bray
Producer: Anthony Hinds
Screenplay: Jimmy Sangster, additional dialogue by Hurford Janes
Photography: Jack Asher
Supervising editor: James Needs
Production designer: Bernard Robinson
Music: Leonard Salzedo
Cast: Peter Cushing (Victor Stein/Frankenstein), Francis Matthews (Dr Hans Kleve), Eunice Gayson (Margaret), Michael Gwynn (Karl), John Welsh (Bergman), Lionel Jeffries (Fritz), Oscar Quitak (Dwarf), Richard Wordsworth (Up Patient), Charles Lloyd Pack (President), John Stuart (Inspector), Arnold Diamond (Molke), Margery Gresley (Countess Barscynska), Anna Walmsley (Vera Barscynska), George Woodbridge (Janitor), Michael Ripper (Kurt), Ian Whittaker (Boy), Avril Leslie (Girl)

The Hound of the Baskervilles 1959, 87 min.

Production company: Hammer
Studio: Bray
Producer: Anthony Hinds
Screenplay: Peter Bryan
Photography: Jack Asher
Supervising editor: James Needs
Production designer: Bernard Robinson
Music: James Bernard
Cast: Peter Cushing (Sherlock Holmes), Andre Morell (Dr Watson), Christopher Lee (Sir Henry), Marla Landi (Cecile), David Oxley (Sir Hugo), Francis de Wolff (Dr Mortimer), Miles Malleson (Bishop), Ewen Solon (Stapleton), John Le Mesurier (Barrymore), Helen Goss (Mrs Barrymore), Sam Kydd (Perkins), Michael Hawkins (Lord Caphill), Judi Moyens (Servant Girl), Michael Mulcaster (Convict), David Banks (Servant)

The Man Who Could Cheat Death 1959, 83 min.

Production company: Hammer
Studio: Bray
Producer: Anthony Hinds
Screenplay: Jimmy Sangster from Barre Lyndon's play *The Man in Half Moon Street*
Photography: Jack Asher
Supervising editor: James Needs
Production designer: Bernard Robinson
Music: Richard Bennett
Cast: Anton Diffring (Georges), Hazel Court (Janine), Christopher Lee (Pierre), Arnold Marle (Ludwig), Delphi Lawrence (Margo), Francis de Wolff (Legris), Gerda Larsen (Street Girl)

The Mummy 1959, 88 min.

Production company: Hammer
Studio: Bray (with additional material shot at Shepperton)
Producer: Michael Carreras
Screenplay: Jimmy Sangster
Photography: Jack Asher

Supervising editor: James Needs
Production designer: Bernard Robinson
Music: Franz Reizenstein
Cast: Peter Cushing (John Banning), Christopher Lee (The Mummy/
   Kharis), Yvonne Furneaux (Isobel/Ananka), Eddie Byrne (Inspector
   Mulrooney), Felix Aylmer (Stephen Banning), Raymond Huntley
   (Joseph Whemple), George Pastell (Mehemet Bey), Michael
   Ripper (Poacher), George Woodbridge (Police Constable), Harold
   Goodwin (Pat), Denis Shaw (Mike), Gerald Lawson (Irish Customer),
   Willoughby Gray (Dr Reilly), John Stuart (Coroner), David Browning
   (Police Sergeant), Frank Sieman (Bill), Stanley Meadows (Attendant),
   Frank Singuineau (Head Porter)

The Stranglers of Bombay 1959, 80 min.

Production company: Hammer
Studio: Bray
Producer: Anthony Hinds
Screenplay: David Z. Goodman
Photography: Arthur Grant
Supervising editor: James Needs
Production designer: Bernard Robinson
Music: James Bernard
Cast: Guy Rolfe (Lewis), Allan Cuthbertson (Connaught-Smith),
   Andrew Cruickshank (Henderson), Marne Maitland (Patel Shari),
   Jan Holden (Mary), George Pastell (High Priest), Paul Stassino
   (Silver), David Spenser (Gopali), Tutte Lemkow (Ram Das), Roger
   Delgado (Bundar), John Harvey (Burns), Michael Nightingale
   (Flood), Marie Devereux (Karim)

The Two Faces of Dr Jekyll 1960, 88 min.

Production company: Hammer
Studio: Bray (with additional material shot at Elstree)
Producer: Michael Carreras
Screenplay: Wolf Mankowitz
Photography: Jack Asher
Supervising editor: James Needs
Production designer: Bernard Robinson
Music and songs: Monty Norman and David Heneker

Cast: Paul Massie (Jekyll/Hyde), Dawn Addams (Kitty), Christopher Lee (Paul Allen), David Kossoff (Litauer), Francis de Wolff (Inspector), Norma Marla (Maria), Magda Miller (Sphinx Girl), William Kendall (Clubman), Helen Goss (Nannie) plus an uncredited appearance by Oliver Reed as a nightclub customer.

The Brides of Dracula 1960, 85 min.

Production company: Hammer
Studio: Bray
Producer: Anthony Hinds
Screenplay: Jimmy Sangster, Peter Bryan and Edward Percy
Photography: Jack Asher
Supervising editor: James Needs
Production designer: Bernard Robinson
Music: Malcolm Williamson
Cast: Peter Cushing (Dr Van Helsing), Martita Hunt (Baroness Meinster), Yvonne Monlaur (Marianne), Freda Jackson (Greta), David Peel (Baron Meinster), Miles Malleson (Dr Tobler), Henry Oscar (Herr Lang), Mona Washbourne (Frau Lang), Andree Melly (Gina), Victor Brooks (Hans), Fred Johnson (Curé), Michael Ripper (Coachman), Norman Pierce (Landlord), Vera Cook (Landlord's wife), Marie Devereux (Village Girl), Michael Mulcaster (Latour)

The Sword of Sherwood Forest 1960, 80 min.

Production company: Hammer/Yeoman
Studio: Ardmore Studios, Ireland
Producer: Sidney Cole and Richard Greene
Screenplay: Alan Hackney
Photography: Ken Hodges
Editor: James Needs
Art director: John Stoll
Music: Alun Hoddinott
Cast: Richard Greene (Robin Hood), Peter Cushing (Sheriff of Nottingham), Niall McGinnis (Friar Tuck), Richard Pasco (The Earl of Newark), Jack Gwillim (Hubert Walter, Archbishop of Canterbury), Sarah Branch (Maid Marian), Nigel Green (Little John), Vanda Godsell (Prioress), Edwin Richfield (Sheriff's Lieutenant), Charles Lamb (Old Bowyer), Dennis Lotis (Allan A' Dale);

uncredited – Derren Nesbitt (Martin), Richard Crean (Ollerton), Oliver Reed (Melton), Adam Kean (Retford), James Neylin (Roger)

The Curse of the Werewolf 1961, 88 min.

Production company: Hammer
Studio: Bray
Producer: Anthony Hinds
Screenplay: John Elder
Photography: Arthur Grant
Supervising editor: James Needs
Production designer: Bernard Robinson
Music: Benjamin Frankel
Cast: Clifford Evans (Alfredo), Oliver Reed (Leon), Yvonne Romain (Servant Girl), Catherine Feller (Cristina), Anthony Dawson (The Marques Siniestro), Josephine Llewellyn (The Marquesa), Richard Wordsworth (The Beggar), Hira Talfrey (Teresa), Justin Walters (Young Leon), John Gabriel (The Priest), Warren Mitchell (Pepe Valiente), Anne Blake (Rosa Valiente), George Woodbridge (Dominique), Michael Ripper (Old Soak), Ewen Solon (Don Fernando), Peter Sallis (Don Enrique), Martin Matthews (Jose), David Conville (Rico Gomez), Denis Shaw (Gaoler), Charles Lamb (Chef), Serafina di Leo (Senora Zumara), Sheila Brennan (Vera), Joy Webster (Isabel), Renny Lister (Yvonne)

The Phantom of the Opera 1962, 84 min.

Production company: Hammer
Studio: Bray
Producer: Anthony Hinds
Screenplay: John Elder, from the novel (or the composition as the film credits put it) by Gaston Leroux
Photography: Arthur Grant
Supervising editor: James Needs
Production designer: Bernard Robinson
Music: Edwin Astley
Cast: Herbert Lom (The Phantom/Professor Petrie), Heather Sears (Christine), Edward De Souza (Harry), Thorley Walters (Latimer), Michael Gough (Ambrose), Harold Goodwin (Bill), Martin Miller (Rossi), Liane Aukin (Maria), Sonya Cordeau (Yvonne), Marne

Maitland (Xavier), Miriam Karlin (Charwoman), Patrick Troughton (Ratcatcher), Renee Houston (Mrs Tucker), Keith Pyott (Weaver), John Harvey (Sergeant Vickers), Michael Ripper (1st Cabby), Miles Malleson (2nd Cabby), Ian Wilson (Dwarf)

Sherlock Holmes und das Halsband des Todes 1962, 86 min.

(co-directed – according to the credits at least – by Frank Winterstein)
Production company: CCC (Berlin)/ Criterion Film (Paris)/ INCEI Film (Rome)
Studio: CCC Studios, Berlin
Producer: Artur Brauner
Screenplay: Curt Siodmak
Photography: Richard Angst
Editor: Ira Oberberg
Art Director: Paul Markwitz
Music: Martin Slavin
Cast: Christopher Lee (Sherlock Holmes), Thorley Walters (Dr Watson), Hans Söhnker (Professor Moriarty), Hans Nielsen (Inspector Cooper), Senta Berger (Ellen Blackburn), Ivan Desny (Paul King), Wolfgang Lukschy (Peter Blackburn), Leon Askin (Charles), Edith Schutlze-Westrum (Mrs Hudson), Bernard Lajarrige (French Police Inspector), Bruno Panthel, Heinrich Gies, Linda Sini, Roland Armontel, Danielle Argence, Franco Giacobini, Waldermar Frahm, Renate Hütter, Max Strassberg

The Horror of It All 1964, 75 min.

Production company: Lippert
Producer: Robert L. Lippert
Screenplay: Ray Russell
Photography: Arthur Lavis
Editor: Robert Winter
Art director: Harry White
Music: Douglas Gamley
Cast: Pat Boone (Jack Robinson), Erica Rogers (Cynthia), Dennis Price (Cornwallis), Andree Melly (Natalia), Valentine Dyall (Reginald), Jack Bligh (Percival), Erik Chitty (Grandpapa), Archie Duncan (Muldoon), Oswald Lawrence (Young Doctor)

The Gorgon 1964, 83 min.

Production company: Hammer
Studio: Bray
Producer: Anthony Nelson Keys
Screenplay: John Gilling (with an uncredited rewrite by Anthony Hinds), from an original story by J. Llewellyn Devine
Photography: Michael Reed
Supervising editor: James Needs
Production designer: Bernard Robinson
Music: James Bernard
Leading players: Peter Cushing (Dr Namaroff), Christopher Lee (Professor Meister), Richard Pasco (Paul Heitz), Barbara Shelley (Carla Hoffmann), Michael Goodliffe (Professor Heitz), Patrick Troughton (Kanof), Jack Watson (Ratoff), Jeremy Longhurst (Bruno Heitz), Toni Gilpin (Sascha), Redmond Phillips (Hans), Joseph O'Conor (Coroner), Alister Williamson (Cass), Joyce Hemson (Martha), Michael Peake (Policeman), Sally Nesbitt (Nurse), Prudence Hyman (Chatelaine – a lady of the castle. This is, of course, a sly joke. In fact she plays Megaera.)

The Earth Dies Screaming 1964, 62 min.

Production company: Lippert
Studio: Shepperton
Producer: Robert L. Lippert
Screenplay: Henry Cross
Photography: Arthur Lavis
Supervising editor: Robert Winter
Art director: George Provis
Music: Elisabeth Lutyens
Cast: Willard Parker (Jeff Nolan), Virginia Field (Peggy), Dennis Price (Taggart), Thorley Walters (Otis), Vanda Godsell (Violet), David Spenser (Mel), Anna Palk (Lorna)

Dracula – Prince of Darkness 1966, 90 min.

Production company: Hammer
Studio: Bray
Producer: Anthony Nelson Keys

Screenplay: John Sansom (Jimmy Sangster)
Photography: Michael Reed
Supervising editor: James Needs
Production designer: Bernard Robinson
Music: James Bernard
Cast: Christopher Lee (Dracula), Barbara Shelley (Helen), Andrew Keir (Father Sandor), Francis Matthews (Charles), Suzan Farmer (Diana), Charles Tingwell (Alan), Thorley Walters (Ludwig), Philip Latham (Klove), Walter Brown (Brother Mark), George Woodbridge (Landlord), Jack Lambert (Brother Peter), Philip Ray (Priest), Joyce Hemson (Mother), John Maxim (Coach Driver)

Island of Terror 1966, 89 min.

Production company: Planet
Studio: Pinewood
Producer: Tom Blakeley
Screenplay: Edward Andrew Mann and Alan Ramsen
Photography: Reg Wyer
Editor: Thelma Connell
Art director: John St John Earl
Music: Malcolm Lockyer
Cast: Peter Cushing (Dr Stanley), Edward Judd (Dr David West), Carole Gray (Toni Merrill), Eddie Byrne (Dr Landers), Sam Kydd (Constable Harris), Niall MacGinnis (Mr Campbell), James Caffrey (Argyle), Liam Gaffney (Bellows), Roger Heathcote (Dunley), Keith Bell (Halsey), Shay Gorman (Morton), Peter Forbes Robertson (Dr Phillips), Richard Bidlake (Carson), Joyce Hemson (Mrs Bellows), Edward Ogden (Helicopter Pilot)

Frankenstein Created Woman 1967, 86 min.

Production company: Hammer
Studio: Bray
Producer: Anthony Nelson Keys
Screenplay: John Elder
Photography: Arthur Grant
Supervising editor: James Needs
Production designer: Bernard Robinson
Music: James Bernard

Cast: Peter Cushing (Baron Frankenstein), Susan Denberg (Christina), Thorley Walters (Doctor Hertz), Robert Morris (Hans), Duncan Lamont (The Prisoner), Peter Blythe (Anton), Barry Warren (Karl), Derek Fowlds (Johann), Alan MacNaughtan (Kleve), Peter Madden (Chief of Police), Philip Ray (Mayor), Ivan Beavis (Landlord), Colin Jeavons (Priest), Bartlett Mullins (Bystander), Alec Mango (Spokesman)

Night of the Big Heat 1967, 94 min.

Production company: Planet
Studio: Pinewood
Producer: Tom Blakeley
Screenplay: Ronald Liles from John Lymington's novel – additional scenes and dialogue by Pip and Jane Baker
Photography: Reg Wyer
Editor: Rod Keys
Art director: Alex Vetchinsky
Music: Malcolm Lockyer
Cast: Christopher Lee (Godfrey Hanson), Patrick Allen (Jeff Callum), Peter Cushing (Dr Vernon Stone), Jane Merrow (Angela Roberts), Sarah Lawson (Frankie Callum), William Lucas (Ken Stanley), Kenneth Cope (Tinker Mason), Percy Herbert (Gerald Foster), Tom Heathcote (Bob Hayward), Anna Turner (Stella Hayward), Jack Bligh (Ben Siddle), Sidney Bromley (Old Tramp), Barry Halliday (Radar Operator)

The Devil Rides Out 1968, 95 min.

Production company: Hammer
Studio: Elstree
Producer: Anthony Nelson Keys
Screenplay: Richard Matheson, from the novel by Dennis Wheatley
Photography: Arthur Grant
Supervising editor: James Needs
Production designer: Bernard Robinson
Music: James Bernard
Cast: Christopher Lee (Duc de Richleau), Charles Gray (Mocata), Niké Arrighi (Tanith), Leon Greene (Rex), Patrick Mower (Simon), Gwen Ffrançon-Davis (Countess), Sarah Lawson (Marie), Paul Eddington (Richard), Rosalyn Landor (Peggy), Russell Waters (Malin)

Frankenstein Must Be Destroyed 1969, 97 min.

Production company: Hammer
Studio: Elstree
Producer: Anthony Nelson Keys
Screenplay: Bert Batt, from a story by Anthony Nelson Keys and Bert Batt
Photography: Arthur Grant
Supervising editor: James Needs
Production designer: Bernard Robinson
Music: James Bernard
Cast: Peter Cushing (Baron Frankenstein), Veronica Carlson (Anna), Freddie Jones (Professor Richter), Simon Ward (Karl), Thorley Walters (Inspector Frisch), Maxine Audley (Ella Brandt), George Pravda (Brandt), Geoffrey Bayldon (Police Doctor), Colette O'Neil (Mad Woman), Frank Middlemass, George Belbin, Norman Shelley, Michael Gover (Guests), Peter Copley (Principal), Jim Collier (Dr. Heidecke), Allan Surtees, Windsor Davies (Police Sergeants), Harold Goodwin (Burglar)

Frankenstein and the Monster from Hell 1974, 99 min.

Production company: Hammer
Studio: Elstree
Producer: Roy Skeggs
Screenplay: John Elder
Photography: Brian Probyn
Editor: James Needs
Art director: Scott MacGregor
Music: James Bernard
Cast: Peter Cushing (Baron Frankenstein), Shane Briant (Simon), Madeline Smith (Sarah), David Prowse (Monster), John Stratton (Asylum Director), Michael Ward (Transvest), Elsie Wagstaff (Wild One), Norman Mitchell (Police Sergeant), Clifford Mollison (Judge), Patrick Troughton (Bodysnatcher), Philip Voss (Ernst), Chris Cunningham (Hans), Charles Lloyd-Pack (Professor Durendel), Lucy Griffiths (Old Kay), Bernard Lee (Tarmut), Sydney Bromley (Muller), Andrea Lawrence (Brassy Girl), Jerold Wells (Landlord), Sheila D'Union (Gerda), Mischa de la Motte (Twitch), Norman Atkyns (Smiler), Victor Woolf (Letch), Winifred Sabine (Mouse), Janet Hargreaves (Chatter), Peter Madden (Coach Driver)

Select bibliography

Material on the British Horror Film and British Cinema which discusses Fisher's work

Dixon, Wheeler Winston, *The Charm of Evil: The Life and Films of Terence Fisher* (Metuchen, NJ and London, Scarecrow Press), 1991.

Fisher, Terence, 'Horror is my business', *Films and Filming*, 10:10 (July 1964), p. 8: an interview with the director.

Hearn, Marcus and Barnes, Alan, *The Hammer Story* (London, Titan), 1997.

Hutchings, Peter, *Hammer and Beyond: The British Horror Film* (Manchester, Manchester University Press), 1993.

Meikle, Dennis, *A History of Horrors: The Rise and Fall of the House of Hammer* (Lanham, MD and London, Scarecrow Press), 1996.

Murphy, Robert, *Sixties British Cinema* (London, BFI), 1992.

Petley, Julian, 'The Lost Continent', in Charles Barr (ed.), *All Our Yesterdays: 90 Years of British Cinema* (London, BFI), 1986.

Pirie, David, *A Heritage of Horror: The English Gothic Cinema 1946–1972* (London, Gordon Fraser), 1973.

Ringel, Harry, 'Terence Fisher: the human side', *Cinefantastique*, 4:3 (1975).

Ringel, Harry, 'Terence Fisher underlining', *Cinefantastique*, 4:3 (1975): an excellent interview with Fisher.

Thomson, David, *A Biographical Dictionary of Cinema* (London, Andre Deutsch), 1994: contains a pithy if rather negative piece on Fisher.

Material relating to British film history that does not discuss Fisher's films in any great detail (if at all) but which provides useful contextual material

Cook, Pam, *Fashioning the Nation: Costume and Identity in British Cinema* (London, BFI), 1996.

Cook, Pam (ed.), *Gainsborough Pictures* (London, Cassell), 1997.

Hutchings, Peter, '"We're the Martians now": British SF invasion fantasies of the 1950s and 1960s', in I. Q. Hunter (ed.), *British Science Fiction Cinema* (London, Routledge), 1999.

McFarlane, Brian, *An Autobiography of British Cinema* (London, Methuen), 1997.

McFarlane, Brian, *Lance Comfort* (Manchester, Manchester University Press), 1999.

MacNab, Geoffrey, *J. Arthur Rank and the British Film Industry* (London, Routledge), 1993.

Miller, David, *The Peter Cushing Companion* (London, Reynolds & Hearn), 2000.

Murphy, Robert (ed.), *The British Cinema Book* (London, BFI), 1997.

Petrie, Duncan, *Creativity and Constraint in the British Film Industry* (London, Macmillan), 1991.

General material on horror which discusses Fisher's work

Auerbach, Nina, *Our Vampires, Ourselves* (Chicago, University of Chicago Press), 1995.

Brosnan, John, *The Horror People* (London, MacDonald & Janes), 1976.

Newman, Kim (ed.), *The BFI Companion to Horror* (London, BFI), 1996.

Pirie, David, *The Vampire Cinema* (London, Galley Press), 1977.

Prawer, S. S., *Caligari's Children: The Film as Tale of Terror* (Oxford, Oxford University Press), 1980.

Waller, Gregory A., *The Living and the Undead: From Stoker's Dracula to Romero's Dawn of the Dead* (Urbana and Chicago, University of Illinois Press), 1986.

Theoretical material relevant to an understanding of Fisher's work

Caughie, John (ed.), *Theories of Authorship* (London, Routledge/BFI), 1981.

Craft, Christopher, '"Kiss me with those red lips"': gender and inversion in Bram Stoker's *Dracula*', in Glennis Byron (ed.), *Dracula* (London, Macmillan), 1999.

Freud, Sigmund, 'The uncanny', in *The Penguin Freud Library – Volume 14: Art and Literature* (Harmondsworth, Penguin), 1990.

Hutchings, Peter, 'Authorship and British cinema – the case of Roy Ward Baker', in Justine Ashby and Andrew Higson (eds), *British Cinema – Past and Present* (London, Routledge), 2000.

Jackson, Rosemary, *Fantasy: The Literature of Subversion* (London, Methuen), 1981.

Willemen, Paul, *Looks and Frictions: Essays in Cultural Studies and Film Theory* (Bloomington and Indianapolis, Indiana University Press), 1994.

Wollen, Peter, *Signs and Meanings in the Cinema* – 3rd edition (London, Secker and Warburg), 1972.

Index